· A FRESH ·

Taste

OF BRITAIN

·

EDITED BY THE
WOMEN'S FARMING UNION

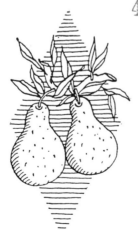

Grub Street · London

Published by Grub Street
Golden House
28–31 Great Pulteney Street
London
W1

Copyright © 1989
Grub Street, London
Text copyright ©
Women's Farming Union
Design Copyright ©
Grub Street, London
Edited by Helen Combe of the WFU,
and Anne Dolamore
Illustrations by Toula Antonakos
Photographs by Tim Imrie

British Library Cataloguing in
Publication Data
A Fresh taste of Britain.
1. Food: British dishes – Recipes
I. Combe, Helen
641.5941

ISBN 0–948817–28–3

Typeset by Chapterhouse,
The Cloisters, Formby
Printed and bound in Great Britain
by Maclehose and Partners,
Portsmouth

CONTENTS

ACKNOWLEDGEMENTS	4
FOREWORD	5
INTRODUCTION	6
ABOUT THE RECIPES	7
GETTING THE BEST FROM YOUR INGREDIENTS	8
SOUPS AND STARTERS	15
MAIN COURSES	29
VEGETABLES AND SALADS	55
HOT AND COLD DESSERTS	60
MENUS FOR SPECIAL OCCASIONS	
CHEF'S CHOICE	68
A FRESH TASTE OF SCOTLAND	72
A FRESH TASTE OF NORTHERN IRELAND	75
A FRESH TASTE OF NORTHERN ENGLAND	78
A FRESH TASTE OF THE MIDLANDS	81
A FRESH TASTE OF THE SOUTHEAST	84
A FRESH TASTE OF THE SOUTHWEST	87
CELEBRATION LUNCHEON	90
SEASONALITY OF BRITISH PRODUCE	93
INDEX	95

ACKNOWLEDGEMENTS

THE COMPETITION AND book were made possible by generous assistance from sixteen organisations representing British farmers and growers. A full list is given below. Dr Megan Slade, Head of Home Economics at Worcester College of Higher Education, gave tremendous help on the technical side of the competition and Daphne MacCarthy's book *Prodfact* (British Food Information Service of Food from Britain) was an invaluable source of reference. To all these and the many others who were involved in or contributed to 'A Fresh Taste of Britain' we say a most sincere 'thank you'.

THE LIST OF SPONSORS

Apple and Pear Development Council
Union House
The Pantiles
Tunbridge Wells
KENT   TN4 8HF

British Egg Information Service
Bury House
126–128 Cromwell Road
Kensington
LONDON   SW7 4ET

British Meat
PO Box 44 Winterhill House
Snowdon Drive
Milton Keynes
MK6 1AX

British Trout Association
PO Box 189
LONDON   SW6 7UT

Farmshop & Pick Your Own Association
Agriculture House
Knightsbridge
LONDON   SW1X 7NJ

Food from Britain
301–344 Market Towers
New Covent Garden Market
LONDON   SW8 5NQ

Milk Marketing Board
Thames Ditton
Surrey   KT7 0EL

Milk Marketing Board for N. Ireland
456 Antrim Road
Belfast
Northern Ireland
BT15 5GD

Mushroom Grower's Association
Agriculture House
Knightsbridge
LONDON   SW1X 7NJ

National Dairy Council
5–7 John Princes Street
LONDON   W1M 0AP

NFU Watercress Association
Agriculture House
Knightsbridge
LONDON   SW1X 7NJ

Potato Marketing Board
50 Hans Crescent
Knightsbridge
LONDON   SW1X 0NB

Quality British Chicken
Bury House
126–128 Cromwell Road
Kensington
LONDON   SW7 4ET

Scottish Food Centre
Motherwell Food Park
Bellshill
Lanarkshire   ML4 3JE

Traditional Farmfresh Turkey Association
5 Beacon Drive
Seaford
E Sussex   BN25 5JX

Welsh Lamb Enterprise Ltd
Brynawel
PO Box 8
Aberystwyth
DYFED   SY23 1DR

Women's Farming Union
Crundalls
Matfield
KENT   TN12 7EA
tel. 089 272 2803

FOREWORD

O NE OF THE most rewarding days of 1989 for me was the Wednesday in March when the six finalists who had been chosen from schools all over the country came together in London to cook their celebration meals for British Food and Farming Year.

Here was a group of very skilled and knowledgeable young people creating from seasonal ingredients a varied range of dishes which confirmed my long held belief that fresh is best.

We are lucky enough in Britain to have a larder of good things and a tradition of regional cooking that has not been completely overwhelmed by the tidal wave of convenience food, and it is to the eternal credit of the Women's Farming Union that they have rallied to the cause of what in these days of highly processed rubbish we must call 'real food'. Being a body of highly intelligent people, the WFU knows that the best and healthiest food comes fresh from the ground and the sea, cooked as simply as possible to accentuate its natural taste and flavour.

In promoting this book they reaffirm their faith in good produce and good home cooking. There is no doubt a role for cans and packets and factory-processed meals but it must always take second place to prime produce freshly prepared. Fortunately for the future health of the nation, more and more schools are alerting their pupils to the vital need for a continuing supply of uncontaminated and nutritious produce from the land.

The WFU are a powerful pressure group in the farming world. Long may they continue to campaign for a responsible approach to the care and conservation of our fields and pastures. Long too may they encourage the provision and preparation of real food for the wellbeing and pleasure of us all.

Derek Cooper

INTRODUCTION

TO FIND THE Celebration Young Cook of the Year was to be the Women's Farming Union's prime contribution to the national Celebration of British Food and Farming. "Will you run it?" I gulped, said "Yes" and thought, "What now?" I talked with a few WFU friends and together we decided to ask Home Economics teachers what kind of competition would appeal to them. With their help 'A Fresh Taste of Britain' was born.

We opened it to 14 and 15 year-old Food and Nutrition students, who were asked to discover foods that were grown or produced locally; to learn how to choose and handle fresh foods and then, selecting the best quality, freshest, regional British foods in season, to produce a three-course celebration meal for four—a meal they would cook for their own families on a special occasion. We also told them they had to cook it in less than 3 hours and that it should cost under £10.

We were overwhelmed by the response. Soon we had to double our print-run of special Project Packs. Teachers welcomed it as the first competition they had seen which looked at the full range of British grown foods. They were particularly interested in the full list of British produce provided by Food from Britain, our major sponsor; some of the students were surprised to learn that 'exotics' such as peppers, aubergines and Kiwi fruit are now grown commercially in Britain—and that oranges and lemons are not.

Running the competition was as much an adventure for us as it obviously was for some of the competitors! A tremendous effort was put in by all who entered, and for this they and their teachers are to be commended—for without them this book would not be possible. The recipes you will find here were all prepared, cooked and tested by the competitors and are family favourites with a regional flavour; but they won't stretch either your time or your pocket. There is a good mix of traditional British cooking with dishes which reflect the growing influence of other culinary cultures, but all of them using British grown ingredients. The eight selected complete menus for that extra special occasion come from the six regional winners themselves, a celebration dinner for the judges of the competition and one chosen by the Chef of the Westbury in London.

Just as our competitors discovered that it is equally important to find the most nutritious, top quality produce as it is to know how to cook it, we hope that you too will discover a fresh taste of Britain through the pages of this book.

Helen Combe, Women's Farming Union

ABOUT THE RECIPES

INGREDIENTS USED THROUGHOUT the book are British, except for essential condiments and spices which cannot be grown here. For this reason, English rapeseed oil has been used as it is the only British vegetable oil. You can of course substitute other oils of your choice if you prefer, but of the vegetable oils, rapeseed has the lowest saturated fat content.

All the recipes are accompanied by the name and school of their creator.

Metric and imperial measurements have been used throughout. Do not mix them.

Where recipes use herbs, amounts given are for fresh herbs. If fresh ones are unavailable the dried equivalent is half or a third. For example, 15 ml (1 tbs) fresh would be equivalent to 5 ml (1 tsp) dried.

Abbreviations used in the book:

tsp	teaspoon	oz	ounce
tbs	tablespoon	pt	pint
g	gram	fl oz	fluid ounce
kg	kilogram	lb	pound
ml	millilitre	in	inch
cm	centimetre		

All recipes (unless otherwise stated) will give four servings.

GETTING THE BEST FROM YOUR INGREDIENTS

MEAT

WHEN SHOPPING

ALL OVER THE country, more and more butchers and retailers are stocking the newer cuts of meat as well as the traditional range. Some of these cuts are extra-lean and many are 'kitchen-ready', a boon if you have little time to spend but want to use fresh ingredients in your cooking. Some farmers are now offering meats produced the traditional way, perhaps organically reared. Ask your butcher, but be prepared to pay more for these specialist products as they cost more to produce.

BEEF

Choose fine-grained lean meat that is firm and red in colour. The colour varies from bright red to reddish brown, but the variations do not affect the quality. Coarser grained meat is better for slow-cooking such as stews and casseroles. Look for a slightly moist appearance. Any beef fat should be firm, dry and creamy yellow. Beef should be aged 10–12 days for best flavour and tenderness. Check with your butcher before buying.

LAMB

Choose fine-grained lean meat that is firm and deep pink in colour. The colour will deepen through the season. Any lamb fat should be crisp and white and the bones pinkish blue in colour.

OFFAL

Freshness is the key word for offal, as it does not keep for more than 2 days (in the fridge). Liver should have little, if any, smell; kidneys and heart should smell and look fresh; sweetbreads should be bright but pale in colour; brains should be pinky-grey. Make sure tongue looks thoroughly clean; feet should look fresh and smell sweet. Oxtail should be bright red with creamy white fat.

PORK
Choose lean meat that is pink in colour and firm.

RABBIT
When buying, look for meat with a good pinkish colour. Rabbit is very lean, but needs a little fat on the tail end and loin.

VENISON
Farmed venison may legally be sold throughout the year, but because of limited supply, most fresh venison is sold between August and January.

POULTRY

CHICKEN AND TURKEY
FRESH POULTRY SHOULD have a plump breast and smooth and pliable legs when bought whole. Some people prefer to buy theirs 'long legged', with head, feet and innards still intact. You can ask your butcher to prepare the bird 'oven-ready' for you.

DUCK
Most fresh duck is sold oven-ready, though it can be found 'fresh-plucked' (needing head, feet and innards removing) in a few specialist outlets. When choosing, make sure both the duck and its packaging is undamaged.

PIGEON
Look for a bird with a plump breast. Available all year round from butchers, supermarkets and specialist game shops.

To Store Meat and Poultry

ALL FRESH MEAT should be covered or loosely wrapped and kept in the coolest part of the fridge for no more than 4 or 5 days. Be careful that it does not drip onto other foods. Be sure to use by the 'best before' date if provided. Poultry should be cooked within 3 days, if stored in a refrigerator; otherwise it should be cooked on the day of purchase. *Cooked meat* should be covered tightly and kept in the coolest part of the fridge for no more than 3 days.

Always read the date stamp on the pack if your purchase is pre-wrapped and choose the freshest samples. Ensure that the pack is undamaged. Look for the British Quality Marks on British Chicken, British Turkey, Charter Bacon, Welsh Lamb and Scotch Quality Beef and Lamb.

FISH

When Shopping

British Trout

FRESH TROUT CAN be bought at the farm gate or from a fishmonger. Supermarkets now stock both fresh and frozen as well as smoked trout. Your fishmonger or the farmer will gut the fish for you if required. Look for bright eyes and a shiny skin. Sunken eyes and loss of bloom indicate the fish is stale.

Scottish Salmon

Look for a fish with a firm, plump body, with a sparkling skin, bright eyes and red gills. Avoid anything with sunken eyes or that which looks flabby. When buying steaks or cutlets try to get them cut from a whole fish of your choice. If not, check that the skin is silvery, the flesh is firm and deep pink, and that it looks freshly cut.

Smoked salmon. Good quality smoked salmon is pink in

colour and the flesh is glossy and dense. Look for the British Quality Mark on Scotch Salmon.

OTHER FISH

Fresh fish will look and smell fresh. Fresh sea-fish will smell of the sea. Look for bright red gills; plenty of bright scales, firmly attached; bright eyes; plump, firm flesh and a moist skin.

SHELLFISH

Buy as fresh as possible, keep in the fridge and cook and use the same day.

NB Any fish or seafood labelled 'do not refreeze' is not fresh. This instruction must be strictly observed.

TO STORE FISH

All fish should be well wrapped and stored in the coldest part of the fridge. Use as quickly as possible, as fresh fish does not keep well.

VEGETABLES AND SALADS

WHEN SHOPPING

WINTER AND SPRING used to be a 'dead' time for British vegetables and salads, with only root crops and brassicas available. But thanks to glasshouses and modern methods of production, the growing season of many other types of vegetables and some salads has been extended. We now even grow 'exotics' such as capsicums (sweet peppers), Chinese leaves and aubergines. Ask your greengrocer if you're not sure if the produce is British—most fruit and vegetables should be labelled with country of origin. Home-produced vegetables, bought fresh, in season, will give the best flavour and will be the best value for money.

For those who want to buy organically-produced vegetables, more British produce is becoming available as growers respond to supply this market. But you will have to pay more for food produced this way and don't be surprised to find

the odd caterpillar or greenfly hiding among the leaves!

Buy frequently and in small quantities, selecting the freshest produce. You cannot buy more freshly than 'picking your own' from a PYO farm.

Be selective. Always check for signs of wilting, damage or bruising and choose the freshest looking samples with good, bright colour. Cut surfaces should be clear and green or white. Look for the British Quality Mark found on some vegetables and salad stuffs.

SOME WAYS TO HELP REDUCE NUTRIENT AND FLAVOUR LOSS

* Light destroys some vitamins, so keep all perishable foods covered, out of light and preferably in the fridge.
* Prepare food just before cooking. Don't leave it standing.
* Wash fruit and vegetables quickly in cold water; do not soak. A salad spinner is very useful.
* Always place vegetables into boiling water and bring back to boiling point as quickly as possible. Do not overcook.
* Vegetable cooking water contains the water soluble vitamins and minerals from the food. Use it for making soups, sauces and gravies. (However, remember always to throw away the water used for cooking pulses, eg, kidney beans.)
* All processing, including cooking, causes mineral loss, so try to eat as much raw salad and fresh fruit as possible.

TO STORE

Root crops. Keep in a cool, dark, dry and airy place.

Greens and salads. Store in the bottom of the fridge, preferably wrapped in a paper bag inside a plastic bag. Some salad stuffs, like watercress and lettuce are best washed, dried and stored in a sealed plastic box in the fridge.

FRESH HERBS

COMMERCIAL GROWERS ARE producing a wide range of fresh herbs. Ask your greengrocer or supermarket for the varieties you want. Keep fresh herbs in the salad drawer of the fridge and use within one or two days.

FRUIT

TOP FRUIT (APPLES, PEARS, PLUMS, ETC)

FRUIT BRUISES EASILY, so it is often cell or tray packed by growers, where each fruit has its own compartment in the box, reducing the risk of bruising in transit from farm to shop. All fruit must be clean and free from blemishes and must conform, however grown, to European Commission grading standards.

WHEN SHOPPING

Be selective. Avoid buying fruit that is bruised or otherwise damaged. Treat it gently—don't put fruit at the bottom of your basket or trolley or load other groceries on top. It bruises very easily. Treat it gently as you do your eggs.

Buy your fruit little and often. If apples are woolly in texture, they have been too long in the shop. Although great care has been taken to bring the apples and pears to you in perfect condition, you may still find bruised and damaged samples occasionally. The Women's Farming Union is one voluntary body checking on quality in association with wholesalers and retailers.

For a wider choice of fruit, try Pick Your Own and farmshop outlets, where many lesser known varieties are available.

TO STORE

Keep **apples** in a cool place—the larder or bottom of the fridge. Buy small quantities frequently to enjoy them at their best. Don't put apples in a bowl in a warm room, or keep them in plastic bags—they will become soft and woolly.

Pears. As pears bruise easily they should be handled carefully. Buy before they are fully ripe and ripen in a warm place such as an airing cupboard. Once ripe, the pear will yield to gentle pressure at the stem end.

SOFT BERRY FRUITS

WHEN SHOPPING

S OFT FRUITS ARE best picked and eaten the same day. Be careful if buying after wet weather as the fruit quickly goes mouldy. Avoid containers that are stained at the base; the bottom layer of fruit could be squashed. Handle all soft fruit carefully as it bruises easily.

TO STORE

Keep all soft fruit cool, preferably in a fridge, and use as quickly as possible.

PICKING STRAWBERRIES

The Farm Shop and Pick Your Own Association gives the following useful advice:

Fruit is likely to be well picked over at the near end of the field. It is worth walking further along the row.

The largest and best berries usually grow to the outside edge of the plants, so walk or kneel carefully between the rows to avoid trampling the crops. Much of the fruit lies hidden. If you brush the leaves aside, you will see the berry clusters below.

While holding the berry carefully in one hand, pinch the stem of a berry between thumb and forefinger, snapping it off above the fruit. Do not attempt to pull the fruit off the stem as soft fruit keeps much better picked with the stem still on.

PICKING RASPBERRIES

Be prepared for a search as the berries may be hidden behind leaves. Select and pick berries that are fully swollen, of good colour, but not too dark. Handle the fruit carefully as it bruises easily.

Soups and Starters

~

Harvest Soup

1 medium onion
1 large leek
2 large carrots
1 large potato
1 large parsnip
4 celery sticks
¼ medium cabbage
25 g (1 oz) butter

5 ml (1 tsp) fresh basil, chopped
1 bay leaf
30 ml (2 tbs) flour
1.2 litres (2 pt) chicken stock
450 g (1 lb) tomatoes
60 ml (4 tbs) parsley, chopped
salt and pepper, to taste

CHOP THE ONION; trim, wash and slice the leek; dice the carrots, potato, parsnip and celery and shred the cabbage keeping it separate. Melt the butter in a saucepan. Add the basil and bay leaf and all the vegetables except the tomatoes, cabbage and parsley. Cook, stirring frequently, for 4 minutes until the onion is softened slightly. Stir in the flour, then gradually pour in the stock, stirring all the time. Bring to the boil, then reduce the heat, cover the pan and simmer for 25 minutes. While soup is simmering, put the tomatoes in a large bowl and pour on boiling water to cover. Leave for a minute or two, drain and peel. Cut the tomatoes into quarters, discard the seeds, and roughly chop. Add the chopped cabbage, tomatoes and parsley to the soup and simmer for a further 10 minutes until the vegetables are tender.

KAREN WADE, ARTHUR MELLOWS VILLAGE COLLEGE, PETERBOROUGH, CAMBRIDGESHIRE

TOMATO SOUP

2 bacon slices, diced
12.5 g (½ oz) butter
2 large onions, sliced
4–6 ripe tomatoes peeled and
   chopped
5 ml (1 tsp) tomato puree
900 ml (1½ pt) chicken stock
parsley
thyme
basil
salt and pepper, to taste

Garlic croutons
1 garlic clove
3 slices white bread
rapeseed oil
cayenne pepper

To garnish
chopped basil, parsley,
   garlic croutons

HEAT THE BACON in a pan until the fat runs. Add butter. When butter has melted, add onions and cook gently for five minutes until tender and golden brown. Add all other ingredients apart from garnish, and cook until tomatoes are tender. Put soup in blender and blend for about 20 minutes or until smooth. Adjust seasoning garnish with basil and parsley and serve hot with croutons.

To prepare garlic croutons

Crush garlic. Remove crusts from bread and cut bread into cubes. Heat oil and when hot, add bread cubes and cook until they start to change colour. Add garlic and mix well. When cubes are golden brown, remove and drain. Sprinkle with salt, pepper and cayenne pepper.

GAIL HENRY, LORD DIGBY'S SCHOOL, SHERBORNE, DORSET

•

A fresh taste of the Southwest

Susan's stuffed eggs; Verwood vegetable pancakes with Cheddar cheese sauce; Clovelly apple and celery salad; Devonshire fruit parcels with clotted cream. Photograph sponsored by the Apple and Pear Development Council.

VEGETABLE AND BEAN SOUP

15 ml (1 tbs) rapeseed oil
1 onion, peeled and thinly
  sliced
1 garlic clove, peeled and
  crushed
8 tomatoes, peeled and
  chopped
45 ml (3 tbs) tomato puree
1 large leek, sliced
600 ml (1 pt) vegetable or
  chicken stock
3 celery sticks, trimmed and
  finely chopped

2 potatoes, scrubbed and finely
  chopped
125 g (4 oz) green beans,
  topped, tailed and coarsely
  chopped
60 ml (4 tbs) fresh broad beans
30 ml (2 tbs) fresh parsley,
  chopped
salt and pepper, to taste

HEAT THE OIL in a saucepan, add the onion and cook gently for 3 minutes until soft but not brown. Add the garlic, tomatoes, tomato puree, leek and stock. Bring to the boil, lower the heat and simmer for 5 minutes. Add the celery, potatoes, green beans, broad beans and parsley. Simmer for 10 minutes until the vegetables are just tender. Add seasoning. Heat through and serve with wholemeal crusty bread.

GILLIAN McDEVITTE, BELFAST ROYAL ACADEMY, BELFAST, COUNTY ANTRIM

•

Celebration luncheon
Stilton and pear flan; Lakeland trout fillets with mushroom stuffing served with Stir-braised carrots and cauliflower; Flame on ice. Photograph sponsored by the British Trout Association.

CHICKEN AND SWEETCORN SOUP

30 ml (2 tbs) rapeseed oil
1 large onion, finely chopped
¼ chicken, skinned, boned and
　chopped
1 carrot, thinly sliced
15 ml (1 tbs) fresh chopped
　mixed herbs (eg, parsley,
　marjoram)

1.2 litres (2 pt) chicken stock
425 g (15 oz) sweetcorn kernels
salt and freshly ground pepper,
　to taste

HEAT THE OIL in a large saucepan. Gently fry the onion until soft. Add the chopped chicken and carrot, and cook until meat is lightly browned. Stir in the herbs and seasoning to taste. Stir in about 300 ml (½ pt) of the stock and bring to the boil. Simmer for 2–3 minutes. Add remaining stock. Bring to the boil; reduce heat to low and simmer for about 20 minutes. Add sweetcorn and simmer for a further 10 minutes. Serve with melba toast.

ELIZABETH APPLEBY, BRINE LEAS HIGH SCHOOL, NANTWICH, CHESHIRE

CUMBRIAN FARE

225 g (8 oz) boned chicken
   breast
50 g (2 oz) Cumberland ham,
   chopped
5 ml (1 tsp) whole grain
   mustard
5 ml (1 tsp) fresh sage, chopped
175 g (6 oz) Cumberland
   sausage
50 g (2 oz) hard goat's cheese
any combination of salad
   ingredients (eg, cucumber,
   lettuce, celery, cress, raw
   cabbage)
salt and black pepper, to taste

Dressing
30 ml (2 tbs) natural yogurt,
15 ml (1 tbs) mayonnaise,
15 ml (1 tbs) chopped chives, all
   mixed together

**Alternative stuffings
for the chicken**
75 g (3 oz) Cumberland sausage
   meat
      or
75 g (3 oz) Cumberland sausage
   meat
5 ml (1 tsp) mixed herbs
      or
75 g (3 oz) breadcrumbs
a little lemon rind
pinch of herbs or parsley
      or
50 g (2 oz) mushrooms
50 g (2 oz) breadcrumbs, little
   chopped onion, all fried
   together

PREHEAT THE OVEN to 200°C (400°F) Gas Mark 6. Cut a pocket in the side of the chicken and fill with ham and mustard mixed together. Secure openings with cocktail sticks. Brush the chicken with oil and sprinkle with sage, black pepper and salt. Cook for 8 minutes or until tender.

Grill the sausage or cook in the oven until golden brown. Cut the cheese to matchsticks. Cool the sausage and chicken. Prepare vegetables for the salad. Mix together all the ingredients for the dressing and pour over the salad. Arrange slices of stuffed chicken, sausage, matchsticks of cheese and salad ingredients on individual dishes.

MARY BURROUGH, COCKERMOUTH SCHOOL, COCKERMOUTH, CUMBRIA

CULLEN SKINK

1 leek
30 ml (2 tbs) butter
350 g (12 oz) smoked haddock,
   cut into small pieces
1 potato, diced
1 bay leaf
300 ml (½ pt) water

300 ml (½ pt) semi-skimmed
   milk
15 ml (1 tbs) flour
salt and cayenne pepper, to
   taste
parsley, to garnish

CHOP THE WHITE part of the leek and soften in 15 ml
(1 tbs) butter. Add the haddock, the diced potato and bay
leaf. Pour in the water and milk. Mix the flour and remaining
butter together with a fork then add to the liquid, a little at a
time. Bring to the boil, stirring constantly. Reduce heat, cover
the pan and simmer 20–25 minutes. Add salt and cayenne
pepper to taste. Scatter over some chopped parsley and serve.

*'Skink' means stock or broth, and this thick and creamy soup is hearty
enough for the coldest of nights.*

ANGELA MACDONALD, DUNOON GRAMMAR SCHOOL, DUNOON, ARGYLL

•

SCALLOP SURPRISE

25 g (4 oz) cod fillet, skinned
225 g (8 oz) potatoes
15 ml (1 tbs) milk
25 g (1 oz) butter
50 g (2 oz) English Cheddar
   cheese

salt and pepper, to taste
sprig of parsley or watercress, to
   garnish
For serving: 4 scallop shells

PLACE THE FISH in a grill pan. Grill until cooked and set
aside. Peel potatoes and cut into quarters. Place potatoes in
saucepan, cover with water and add a pinch of salt. Boil until

tender, drain and mash with milk, butter and the cheese, saving a little cheese for the topping. Flake the fish, season and place in the bottom of each scallop shell. Cover the fish with the potato mix and sprinkle the remaining cheese on top. Place under the grill until the cheese is melted. Place a sprig of fresh parsley or watercress on top to garnish.

NATASHA WYETH, INVICTA GRAMMAR SCHOOL FOR GIRLS, MAIDSTONE, KENT

•

VEGETABLE AND FISH KEBABS

12 baby onions
275 g (10 oz) aubergine
275 g (10 oz) courgettes
1 red pepper, chopped
12 button mushrooms
4 cod fillets cut into bite-sized
  pieces

30 ml (2 tbs) lemon juice
30 ml (2 tbs) chopped mixed
  fresh herbs
2 garlic cloves, crushed
2.5 ml ($\frac{1}{2}$ tsp) ground ginger
1.25 ml ($\frac{1}{4}$ tsp) ground turmeric
5 ml (1 tsp) ground cumin

Marinade
120 ml (8 tbs) English rapeseed
  oil

COOK ONIONS IN boiling water for 5 minutes, drain and remove skins. Cut the aubergine and courgettes into 2.5 cm (1 in) chunks. Mix the marinade ingredients together in a large bowl, add all the vegetables and toss well. Leave for 15 minutes to 1 hour. Thread the fish and the vegetables onto 8 long skewers. Cook under a moderately heated grill for about 8 minutes, turning over half way through. Serve immediately.

LISA CLARK, CHRIST'S HOSPITAL, HORSHAM, WEST SUSSEX

SHRIMPS BAKED IN SOUR CREAM

225 g (8 oz) shrimps
150 ml (5 fl oz) sour cream
50 g (2 oz) fresh wholemeal
   breadcrumbs

50 g (2 oz) Cheshire cheese,
   grated
50 g (2 oz) butter
salt and black pepper, to taste

P REHEAT THE OVEN to 150°C (300°F) Gas Mark 2.
Divide the shrimps between four small ovenproof dishes.
Season well and cover with cream. Sprinkle breadcrumbs and
cheese on top, dot with knobs of butter and bake in the oven
for 10 minutes.

NIKKI ANNISON, SHAVINGTON HIGH SCHOOL, CREWE, CHESHIRE

•

SMOKED TROUT PATE

2 smoked trout
25 g (1 oz) English butter
1.25 ml ($\frac{1}{4}$ tsp) cayenne pepper
50 g (2 oz) cream cheese

5 ml (1 tsp) fresh parsley,
   chopped
ground black pepper, to taste

R EMOVE SKIN AND bones from the trout and flake the
fish into a basin. Add the butter and mash with a wooden
spoon or blend until smooth. Add seasoning. Stir in the cream
cheese and parsley and mix thoroughly, blending again if
necessary. Transfer pate into a loaf dish and chill for at least 1
hour. Serve sliced with melba toast.

CLAIRE MITCHELL, OXENFOORD CASTLE SCHOOL, PATHHEAD, MIDLOTHIAN

SMOKED MACKEREL WITH APPLE

125 g (4 oz) celery
125 g (4 oz) cucumber
125 g (4 oz) red eating apple
   (Discovery or Spartan), cored
350 g (12 oz) smoked mackerel
150 ml ($\frac{1}{4}$ pt) plain yogurt

30 ml (2 tbs) lemon juice
paprika, to taste
1 small crisp lettuce
lemon wedges, to garnish
   (optional)

FINELY CHOP CELERY, cucumber and apple. Skin fish and flake flesh roughly with a fork. Discard bones. Combine celery, cucumber, apple and mackerel in a bowl. Stir in yogurt, lemon juice and paprika to taste. Shred lettuce on a board with a sharp knife. Place a little lettuce in the bases of 4 stemmed glasses. Divide the mackerel mixture equally between them. Garnish each glass with a lemon wedge if desired, and a sprinkle of paprika. Serve at room temperature, with crusty bread or as part of a light salad lunch.

MELISSA GUNN, TONBRIDGE GRAMMAR SCHOOL FOR GIRLS, TONBRIDGE, KENT

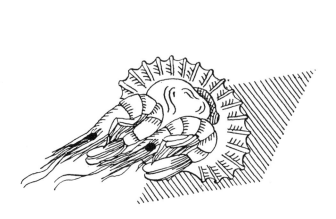

BABY CORN COB FLOWERS

16 baby corn on the cob
1 small lettuce
2 tomatoes

Dressing
30 ml (2 tbs) mayonnaise
30 ml (2 tbs) plain yogurt

BOIL THE SWEETCORN in salted boiling water until soft,
drain and leave covered with a lid. Wash and dry four
lettuce leaves and two tomatoes. Slice the tomatoes in half.
Place the leaves on four plates with half a tomato in the
middle. Place the sweetcorn-like petals round the tomato and
serve, with a dressing of mayonnaise and plain yogurt mixed
together.

*A colourful starter and a lot of fun, because you can eat it petal by petal
until you are left with the lettuce leaf.*

TRACEY DELPRATT, CHALLNEY GIRLS' HIGH, LUTON, BEDFORDSHIRE

•

CHEESE CAROUSEL

125 g (4 oz) Cheshire cheese,
  grated
225 g (8 oz) cottage cheese
4 thick slices of ham
mixed herbs (eg, parsley, basil),
  to taste
4 thick slices of ham

Salad platter
1 red pepper
1 green pepper

few spring onions or 1 whole
  onion
$\frac{1}{4}$ red cabbage
$\frac{1}{4}$ Iceberg lettuce

Garnish
4 small sticks of cheese
fresh herbs, chopped
1 tomato
1 slice cucumber

MIX THE CHESHIRE cheese with the cottage cheese and sprinkle in some mixed herbs to add colour and flavour. Make the ham into cornets and fill with the cheese mixture. Place them on a plate in a star shape with pointed ends towards the centre. Wash and prepare the salad ingredients. Slice the peppers, chop the onion into rings or slices and shred the cabbage and lettuce. Arrange lettuce between cornets and mix the remaining salad ingredients together and use to garnish on top of the lettuce. Place a cheese stick in the end of each cornet and sprinkle with herbs. Put the tomato, cut into quarters, and the cucumber slice in the centre.

JOANNE TAYLOR, HARTFORD HIGH SCHOOL, NORTHWICH, CHESHIRE

•

MUSHROOM PATE

1 onion, sliced
1 garlic clove, crushed
25 g (1 oz) butter
350 g (12 oz) mushrooms, chopped (1 mushroom for garnish)

175 g (6 oz) low fat cream cheese
salt and pepper, to taste
4 small sprigs watercress, to garnish

FRY ONION AND garlic in the butter until soft. Add mushrooms and fry until soft. Cool, drain off liquid. Puree mushrooms with other ingredients in a food processor or blender. Season to taste and spoon into four small earthenware or china pots. Chill till firm. Garnish with a sprig of watercress and one slice of mushroom. Serve with melba toast.

MARIA WATTS, MOUNT GRACE SCHOOL, POTTERS BAR, HERTS

25

BREADED MUSHROOMS WITH GARLIC SAUCE

12 medium-sized mushrooms
seasoned flour
1 egg
40 g (1½ oz) wholewheat
   breadcrumbs
rapeseed oil, for frying

Garlic sauce
1 garlic clove
25 g (1 oz) English butter
25 g (1 oz) plain flour
300 ml (½ pt) milk
salt and pepper, to taste
cress, to garnish

WASH, THEN WIPE the mushrooms and trim stalks. Cover the mushrooms with some seasoned flour. Beat the egg, then coat the mushrooms. Roll in a good covering of breadcrumbs. Then put to one side to prepare the sauce. Place all ingredients for the sauce into a blender and blend for thirty seconds. Transfer to a saucepan and bring to a boil for 2 minutes, stirring constantly. Season to taste with salt and pepper and cover. Fry mushrooms until golden brown. Place mushrooms on 4 small tea plates with a spoonful of sauce and garnish with cress.

KIRSTY GILHAM, GREENSWARD SCHOOL, HOCKLEY, ESSEX

PEARS AND CURD CHEESE

50 g (2 oz) Blue Stilton cheese,
  crumbled
150 g (5 oz) natural yogurt
125 g (4 oz) fromage frais

2 Comice pears
lemon juice
lettuce leaves

MASH THE STILTON with a little yogurt. Mix together the fromage frais and remaining yogurt. Peel, halve and core the pears, placing each half into water containing lemon juice to stop them going brown. When ready to serve, place each pear half on a bed of lettuce on individual plates and fill with the cheese mixture. Spoon over the fromage frais and yogurt mixture to cover the pear completely, and serve.

STEPHANIE PURNELL, PICARDY SCHOOL, BELVEDERE, KENT

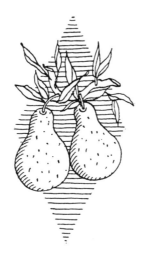

VINNEY PATE WITH PEARS

225 g (8 oz) full fat curd cheese
45 ml (3 tbs) milk
175 g (6 oz) Blue Vinney
 cheese, grated
pinch of nutmeg
4 ripe Comice pears

1 bunch watercress
4 slices lemon
juice of 1 lemon
4 slices of brown bread for
 melba toast

B EAT THE CURD cheese with sufficient milk to give a smooth creamy texture. Stir in Vinney cheese and season with nutmeg. Shape into a roll about 4 cm (1¾ in) in diameter and chill in cling film for at least one hour. Just before serving, peel and slice the pears. Divide pate into four and arrange on four plates with the pears. Garnish with watercress and lemon slices. Cut crusts from the bread, and toast lightly each side. Cut through each slice, toast cut sides, making 8 slices melba toast.

Blue Vinney is a hard white, blue-veined cheese, made from semi-skimmed cow's milk and is only to be found in Dorset. If you are not lucky enough to have this delicious cheese, use another blue cheese, such as Stilton but of course the flavour will not be the same.

JOANNA HARRIS, ST ALDHELMS SCHOOL, SHERBORNE, DORSET

Main Courses

~

SAVOURY CHICKEN

4 chicken breasts, about 175 g
(6 oz) each, skinned, boned
and cut into bite-sized pieces
30 ml (2 tbs) flour, plain
wholemeal
25 g (1 oz) N Ireland butter
30 ml (2 tbs) rapeseed oil
2 onions, skinned and chopped
175 g (6 oz) button
mushrooms, thinly sliced

5 ml (1 tbs) fresh mixed herbs
1 bay leaf
30 ml (2 tbs) fresh parsley,
finely chopped
900 g (2 lb) floury potatoes,
scrubbed and thinly sliced
300 ml ($\frac{1}{2}$ pt) cider
300 ml ($\frac{1}{2}$ pt) chicken stock
salt and pepper, to taste
chopped parsley, to garnish

PREHEAT THE OVEN to 190 °C (375 °F) Gas Mark 5. Toss
chicken pieces in seasoned flour. Heat the butter and oil in
a pan, add the chicken and saute until brown and sealed. Place
in a casserole. Cover with onions, mushrooms, herbs, chopped
parsley and seasoning. Arrange the potato slices neatly over the
top. Pour cider and stock into casserole so the potatoes are just
covered by the liquid. Add extra stock if necessary. Cover and
cook for 1 hour. Remove cover and cook for a further 15
minutes until browned on top. Serve hot, garnished with
chopped parsley. Serve with a large dish of mixed vegetables –
for example, cauliflower, carrots, peas and broad beans.

LORNA CAMPBELL, BELFAST ROYAL ACADEMY, BELFAST, COUNTY ANTRIM

CHICKEN BREASTS WITH GINGER AND GARLIC

125 g (4 oz) spring onions
small cube of fresh ginger
2 garlic cloves, crushed
1 lemon

4 chicken breasts
400 ml (14 fl oz) chicken stock
125 g (4 oz) natural yogurt
salt and pepper, to taste

PEEL AND TRIM the spring onions and set aside 75 g (3 oz). Place the remainder in a food processor with ginger and garlic and process to a rough paste, adding a little water if necessary. If you do not have a food processor, wrap the ginger, garlic and onion in greaseproof paper and beat it on a table top with a heavy pan. Peel zest from the lemon and stir it into the paste.

Skin the chicken breasts and carefully cut the flesh away from the bone with a sharp knife. Spread the paste over the chicken breasts, cover and leave in the refrigerator for about 12 hours, or up to 24 hours. If you are in a hurry, leave them in a cool place for an hour or so.

Pick out pared lemon zest from the mixture and drop it into boiling water for 3 minutes, then cut into fine strips and set aside. Scrape the paste from the chicken and place it in a saucepan with the stock, bring to the boil, cover and simmer for 20 minutes. Strain, pressing hard with a spoon to extract all the liquid.

Preheat the grill to high. Slice the reserved spring onions very finely on the diagonal. Return the strained stock to saucepan and boil for 10–15 minutes until reduced to about 50 ml (2 fl oz). Remove from heat and whisk in the yogurt, a little at a time. Add lemon juice to taste, season if necessary. Add the remaining spring onions and lemon strips. Set aside.

Grill the chicken breasts for 4–5 minutes each side or until they are cooked through, but still moist and slightly spongy.

Return sauce to heat and warm gently adding a little more stock if necessary. Cut the chicken into 1 cm ($\frac{1}{2}$ in) slices, crosswise on the diagonal. Fan the slices out on each dinner plate, spoon the sauce over and serve.

SAMANTHA LORD, CHALLNEY GIRLS' HIGH SCHOOL, LUTON, BEDFORDSHIRE

•

HONEY BARBECUED CHICKEN

50 g (2 oz) English butter
125 g (4 oz) onions, peeled and finely chopped
1 garlic clove, peeled and finely chopped
450 g (1 lb) tomatoes, peeled and chopped
30 ml (2 tbs) Worcestershire sauce

15 ml (1 tbs) honey
4 chicken drumsticks, fresh
salt and freshly ground pepper, to taste
mushrooms, tomatoes and watercress, to garnish

T O MAKE BARBECUE sauce, combine the butter, onions, garlic, tomatoes, Worcestershire sauce, honey, salt and pepper in a saucepan. Cook gently for 30 minutes. Place the chicken drumsticks in the grill pan and brush liberally with the barbecue sauce, grill for 10 minutes on each side, brushing frequently with more sauce. Serve with hot baked potatoes and garnish with grilled mushrooms, tomato slices and watercress. Serve the remaining sauce separately.

CLAIRE ROWLANDS, HARTFORD HIGH SCHOOL, NORTHWICH, CHESHIRE

STUFFED CHICKEN BREASTS

25 g (1 oz) unsalted English
butter
4 chicken breasts, boned and
skinned
125 g (4 oz) Cheshire cheese,
grated
2 garlic cloves, peeled and
crushed
125 g (4 oz) broccoli, cooked
and chopped

mixed herbs: 5 ml (1 tsp) each
fresh chopped parsley, sage
and thyme
salt and pepper, to taste

White sauce
50 g (2 oz) butter
50 g (2 oz) plain flour
600 ml (1 pt) milk

PREHEAT THE OVEN to 200°C (400°F) Gas Mark 6. Grease an ovenproof dish. Melt the butter in a frying pan and lightly fry the chicken breasts on both sides. Allow the meat to cool, then make a slit in each breast and stuff with a mixture of grated cheese and garlic. Wrap each breast in foil and cook for 25 minutes. Make the white sauce by melting the butter, stirring in the flour and then gradually pouring in the milk. When the sauce has thickened add the broccoli and herbs. When the chicken is cooked, place on dish and pour over sauce.

The Cheshire cheese and garlic stuffing adds flavour to the chicken breasts and its creamy texture is a good contrast to the meat. Serve with carrots with lemon and mint, duchesse potatoes, and broccoli.

JAYNE TURNER, NEWCASTLE UNDER LYME SCHOOL, NORTH STAFFS

•

A fresh taste of Northern England
Leek and potato soup; Laversdale lamb accompanied by Potato nests
filled with fresh garden peas; Bramble and apple meringue.
Photograph sponsored by British Meat.

BRITISH MEAT
EDUCATIONAL
SERVICE

HUMBERSIDE CHICKEN BREASTS
(FATHER'S FAVOURITE)

4 slices of lean ham
4 thin slices of Stilton or
   Cheddar cheese
4 chicken breasts
125 g (4 oz) button mushrooms
75 g (3 oz) unsalted English
   butter

15 g ($\frac{1}{2}$ oz) seasoned flour
15 ml (1 tbs) rapeseed oil
150 ml ($\frac{1}{4}$ pt) chicken stock
15 ml (1 tbs) parsley, chopped
freshly ground black pepper, to
   taste

CUT THE HAM and cheese slices to fit the chicken breasts. Trim the mushrooms and slice thinly. Cook until soft in 15 g ($\frac{1}{2}$ oz) of butter. Put aside. Coat the chicken breasts evenly, but not too thickly, with the seasoned flour. Melt the remaining butter and the oil in a large frying pan over moderate heat. Fry the chicken for about 5 minutes on both sides. Place a slice of ham on each chicken breast, spoon over a thin layer of mushrooms and season lightly with freshly ground black pepper. Sprinkle a little of the parsley over the mushrooms and cover with a slice of cheese. Pour the hot stock over the chicken, cover the pan closely and cook over a low heat for about 15 minutes or until the cheese has melted. Lift out the chicken and arrange on a serving dish. Sprinkle over the remaining parsley. Serve with roast potatoes, peas and carrots.

EMMA JONES, MATTHEW HUMBERSTONE COMPREHENSIVE SCHOOL, CLEETHORPES, SOUTH HUMBERSIDE

•

A fresh taste of Northern Ireland
Delia's country surprise; Haddock crumble served with Glazed Derry carrots and Brussels sprouts; Baked apple cheesecake. Photograph sponsored by the Milk Marketing Board for Northern Ireland.

CURRIED CHICKEN AND YOGURT PLAIT

300 ml (½ pt) yogurt
45 ml (3 tsp) curry powder
350 g (12 oz) chicken, cooked and diced
175 g (6 oz) carrots, cooked and diced
1 onion, chopped
350 g (12 oz) rough puff pastry
beaten egg, to glaze
salt and pepper, to taste

Rough puff pastry
75 g (3 oz) lard
75 g (3 oz) English butter
225 g (8 oz) plain flour
2.5 ml (½ tsp) salt
150 ml (¼ pt) cold water
5 ml (1 tsp) lemon juice

To make the pastry

CUT THE LARD and the butter into small pieces. Sieve the flour and salt into a bowl, stir in the fat. Mix the water and lemon juice, add enough of this water to the flour and fat to give a stiff dough. Turn out onto a floured board and gently press the pastry together. Roll out to a long oblong. Fold the top third down and the bottom third up. Turn the pastry round so that the folds are at the side. Roll and fold the pastry three more times, turning the pastry always in the same direction. Chill for 30 minutes. Then roll into an oblong 30 × 35 cm (12 × 14 in).

To make the plait

Preheat oven to 200°C (400°F) Gas Mark 6. Mix together the yogurt, curry powder and seasoning and add chicken, carrots and onion. Place the mixture down the centre of the pastry. Make diagonal cuts in pastry on either side of the filling about 2.5 cm (1 in) apart, and brush edges with egg. Fold the cut pastry strips over the filling, alternating the right side with the left to form a plait, until the filling is completely covered. Tuck in the pastry ends. Carefully put onto a greased baking tray and brush the plait with the egg. Bake in the oven for 30–35 minutes until golden brown.

LISA CLARK, CHRIST'S HOSPITAL, HORSHAM, WEST SUSSEX

•

CHICKEN WITH YOGURT

1 onion
1 garlic clove
1 red pepper
1.5 kg (3 lb 6 oz) chicken
   portions
65 g (2½ oz) flour
600 ml (1 pt) chicken stock

300 ml (½ pt) natural yogurt
salt and pepper, to taste
chopped fresh chives or parsley,
   and red pepper strips, to
   garnish

PEEL THE ONION and garlic; chop the onion and crush the garlic. De-seed the pepper and chop half of it. Cut remainder in strips for garnish. Heat the butter in a flame-proof dish, add chicken pieces and cook until browned all over. Add the onion, pepper and garlic. Sprinkle over the flour and stir for 1 minute. Stir in stock and seasoning. Bring to the boil, lower heat, cover the dish and simmer gently for one hour, until chicken is thoroughly cooked. Remove pan from the heat. Take out the chicken pieces with a slotted spoon, then stir in yogurt to the sauce and adjust seasoning to taste before serving. Sprinkle with chopped chives or parsley and garnish with red pepper strips.

ANNE MUIRHEAD, DENNY HIGH SCHOOL, DENNY, STIRLINGSHIRE

CHICKEN THERESE

4 chicken breasts
15 ml (1 tbs) flour
30 ml (2 tbs) rapeseed oil
1 small onion, chopped
225 g (8 oz) tomatoes, peeled,
  seeded and chopped

225 g (8 oz) mushrooms, sliced
2 celery stalks, chopped
600 ml (1 pt) chicken stock
450 g (1 lb) cauliflower
450 g (1 lb) carrots
salt and black pepper, to taste

PREHEAT THE OVEN to 170°C (325°F) Gas Mark 3. Wash and dry chicken breasts. Dust with the seasoned flour. Fry onions gently in the oil until transparent. Add the chicken breasts and continue frying until chicken is browned and seared. Then add the chopped tomatoes, mushrooms and celery together with stock, bring to boil, put into a casserole dish and cook in the oven for about 1½ hours or until the chicken is tender. Taste and adjust seasoning. Boil the carrots and cauliflower until just tender and serve all together when ready.

KARYN THERESE HAY, HUNTCLIFF COMPREHENSIVE SCHOOL, KIRTON-IN-LINDSEY, LINCOLNSHIRE

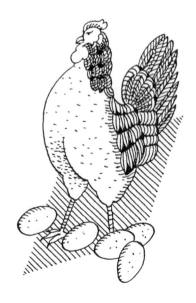

EAST ANGLIAN TURKEY BREASTS WITH ASPARAGUS

225 g (8 oz) thin asparagus
stalks
4 turkey breasts, skinned and
boned
30 ml (2 tbs) plain flour
15 ml (1 tbs) rapeseed oil
15 g ($\frac{1}{2}$ oz) butter

300 ml ($\frac{1}{2}$ pt) chicken stock
5 ml (1 tsp) chopped fresh sage
60 ml (4 tbs) dry English cider
150 ml (5 fl oz) fresh soured
cream
salt and pepper, to taste

CUT OFF THE ends of the asparagus if they are tough and
woody. Trim them all to the same length. Cut off the tips
and cut the stalks into 3 pieces. Beat out the turkey breasts
slightly with a rolling pin or a meat mallet. Coat with seasoned
flour, shaking off any excess. Heat oil and butter in a large
frying pan. Fry the turkey until browned on both sides. Add
the chicken stock, asparagus stalks – reserving the tips – the
sage and cider. Cover and cook gently for 15–20 minutes until
tender. Five minutes before the end of the cooking time, stir in
the reserved asparagus tips, keeping a few back for garnish.
Add soured cream. Season to taste.

DENISE WHITER, GREENSWARD SCHOOL, HOCKLEY, ESSEX

LINCOLNSHIRE ROAST DUCK WITH STUFFING

2 kg (4½ lb) duckling

Sage and onion stuffing
50 g (2 oz) butter
225 g (8 oz) chopped onions
100 g (3½ oz) wholemeal
   breadcrumbs

grated rind of 1 lemon
15 ml (1 tbs) fresh sage
1 egg, beaten
salt and pepper, to taste

To make the stuffing

MELT BUTTER, ADD onions and fry gently for 10 minutes or until tender and lightly browned. Mix with breadcrumbs, lemon rind and sage. Bind together with egg and season.

To cook the duckling

Preheat the oven to 180°C (350°F) Gas Mark 4. Pat duckling dry inside and out with kitchen roll. Damp duck will not crisp easily. Fill cavity with stuffing, securing the opening with small skewers. Prick skin with a skewer or fork to allow the fat to flow. Rub well with salt to help crisp skin. Place duckling, breast side up, on a rack in a roasting pan. Raising the duck ensures drippings drain freely. Roast for 30 minutes per 450 g (1 lb). Increase temperature for last 20 minutes to 200°C (400°F) Gas Mark 6 for a crisp golden finish. Baste the bird from time to time during cooking to keep flesh moist.

Stuffing the duck keeps the duck meat moist and also enhances the flavour of the dish.

EMMA BOWSER, WILLIAM FARR COMPREHENSIVE SCHOOL, WELTON, LINCOLNSHIRE

BEEF OLIVES WITH MUSHROOM STUFFING

8 thin slices of topside
15 g (½ oz) N Ireland butter
15 ml (1 tbs) tomato puree
fresh parsley, finely chopped,
   to garnish

Mushroom stuffing
75 g (3 oz) button mushrooms,
   finely diced

5 ml (1 tsp) mustard
1 carrot, scrubbed and grated
1 courgette, peeled and grated
15 ml (1 tbs) bran
10 ml (2 tsp) tomato puree
450 ml (¾ pt) beef stock
salt and pepper, to taste

PREHEAT THE OVEN to 180°C (350°F) Gas Mark 4. Beat the beef slices between sheets of damp greaseproof paper until almost double in size. For the stuffing mix mushrooms, mustard, salt and pepper, carrot, courgette, bran and 10 ml (2 tsp) tomato puree. Divide mixture between the beef slices and spread over evenly. Roll and secure at both ends with fine string. Melt the butter in a casserole and brown the beef olives. Add seasoning and the stock. Cook for 45 minutes. Transfer meat to serving dish with a slotted spoon and keep hot. Stir in remaining tomato puree to stock and pour over the beef olives. Garnish and serve at once.

GILLIAN McDEVITTE, BELFAST ROYAL ACADEMY, BELFAST, COUNTY ANTRIM

BEEF STEW WITH CELERY AND WALNUTS

675 g (1½ lb) stewing beef
50 g (2 oz) butter
8 small onions or shallots, peeled
25 g (1 oz) wholemeal flour
2 garlic cloves, peeled and crushed
1 bay leaf

600 ml (1 pt) chicken stock
12 walnuts, chopped
1 celery stick, chopped
15 ml (1 tbs) grated orange peel
salt and pepper, to taste

PREHEAT THE OVEN to 170°C (325°F) Gas Mark 3. Cut meat into large cubes, heat butter in large pan and fry meat on all sides. Remove meat, set aside, and fry onions whole until golden. Stir in flour, add meat, crushed garlic, bay leaf and seasoning. Cover with stock. Cook for 1½ – 2 hours until the meat is tender. After 1 hour, fry walnuts and celery and add to the stew. Sprinkle with orange peel before serving.

Walnuts add an unusual and delicious taste to this economical and filling meal.

NIKKI ANNISON, SHAVINGTON HIGH SCHOOL, CREWE, CHESHIRE

KENTISH DELIGHT

675 g (1½ lb) potatoes, peeled
225 g (8 oz) peas
450 g (1 lb) carrots, diced
125 g (4 oz) Bramley cooking apples, peeled and diced

50 g (2 oz) blackberries
4 loin pork chops
15 ml (1 tbs) milk
25 g (1 oz) butter

USING 3 SAUCEPANS, boil potatoes, carrots and peas, and apples and blackberries until all are cooked. Grill the chops. Mash the potatoes with butter and milk, place in a piping bag and pipe swirls on to each plate. Mash the fruit to a pulp and drain off the juice. Spoon pulp over pork chops. Serve with carrots and peas.

NATASHA WYETH, INVICTA GRAMMAR SCHOOL FOR GIRLS, MAIDSTONE, KENT

•

BEEF AND VEGETABLE CASSEROLE

450 g (1 lb) stewing beef
50 g (2 oz) plain flour
2 carrots
2 onions
½ small turnip

30 ml (2 tbs) rapeseed oil
450 ml (¾ pt) beef stock
2 bay leaves
salt and pepper, to taste
parsley sprigs, to garnish

PREHEAT OVEN TO 170°C (325°F) Gas Mark 3. Place shelf in centre of oven. Wipe the meat, remove any excess fat, cut into small cubes and coat in 25 g (1 oz) of seasoned flour. Peel and slice carrots and onions. Peel turnips and cut into cubes. Heat the oil in a pan and fry the meat and vegetables for about 5 minutes. Stir in the rest of the flour. Add stock to the pan and bring to the boil. Adjust seasoning. Pour into a casserole dish, add bay leaves, cover and bake in oven for 1–1½ hours until the meat is tender. Serve sprinkled with a little chopped parsley.

BRENDA TURNER, HIRST HIGH SCHOOL, ASHINGTON, NORTHUMBERLAND

WILTSHIRE PLAIT

250 g (9 oz) minced belly pork
   (lean end) or pork sausage
   meat
½ small cooking apple
1 small onion
1 garlic clove
50 g (2 oz) mature Cheddar
   cheese
1 egg
60–70 ml (4–5 tbs) parsley,
   chopped
salt and black pepper, to taste

Rough puff pastry
175 g (6 oz) plain flour
125 g (4 oz) English butter
pinch salt
175 g (6 oz) iced water
1 egg, beaten
flour

To make the pastry

MIX FLOUR AND salt. Cut butter into cubes and stir into flour. Add water and mould into a firm dough. Pat and roll into a long oblong. Fold the top third down and bottom third up. Turn pastry so folds are at the side. Roll out and repeat twice. Chill before using.

To make the plait

Preheat the oven to 220°C (425°F) Gas Mark 7. Chop and dice apple, cheese, onion and garlic and mix with meat. Add parsley, salt and pepper. Bind with egg. Roll pastry to a 25 cm (10 in) square. Place meat mixture in centre. Cut pastry either side diagonally into strips. Damp ends of strips and fold them alternately from either side over the meat in a plait. Glaze with beaten egg. Cook for 20 minutes. Then reduce heat to 180°C (350°F) Gas Mark 4 for further 20–25 minutes.

JOANNA HARRIS, ST ALDHELMS SCHOOL, SHERBORNE, DORSET

PORK AND PEARS

25 g (1 oz) English butter
4 pork chops, trimmed of rind
   and fat
2 large Conference pears,
   peeled, cored and halved

15 ml (1 tbs) chopped fresh
   marjoram
15 ml (1 tbs) lemon juice
salt and freshly ground pepper,
   to taste

PREHEAT THE OVEN to 190°C (375°F) Gas Mark 5. Melt the butter in a large frying pan. Add the chops and fry gently for 3–4 minutes on each side until golden brown. Remove with a slotted spoon and place in a single layer in a greased ovenproof dish. Sprinkle with salt and pepper to taste. Lightly poach the pears in a little water until just soft. Drain, reserving the juice. Place pear halves cut side down, one on top of each chop in the dish. Pour the reserved pear juice into a pan and stir with a wooden spoon. Add the marjoram and lemon juice. Bring to the boil and boil rapidly, stirring frequently for about 5 minutes until reduced by about half. Pour over the chops and pears, then cover the dish. Bake in the oven for 25 minutes or until the chops are tender. Transfer to a warm serving dish and serve at once.

Pork and pears is a lovely treat for the autumn as pears are in season and will be fresh and readily available. Trimming the chops of fat and rind considerably reduces the fat content of the meat.

SUSANNAH FARR, ELLERSLIE SCHOOL, MALVERN, WORCESTERSHIRE

LINCOLNSHIRE LAMB CASSEROLE

675 g (1½ lb) British shoulder of
   lamb
30 ml (2 tbs) rapeseed oil
2 onions, sliced
4 carrots, cut in thin strips
2 celery sticks, cut in thin strips
300 ml (½ pt) tomato juice

10 ml (2 tsp) ground cumin
1 garlic clove, peeled and
   crushed
125 g (4 oz) mushrooms, sliced
salt, to taste
pinch cayenne pepper

Preheat oven to 170°C (325°F) Gas Mark 3. Cut the lamb into 2.5 cm (1 in) cubes. Brown the lamb in the oil in an oven-proof casserole. Add onions, carrots and celery. Mix the tomato juice, ground cumin, garlic and seasoning and pour over the lamb and vegetables. Cover and cook for 1 hour. Add the mushrooms and cook for a further 30 minutes until the meat is tender. Serve with baked jacket potatoes and green salad.

Any surplus fat may be removed from the surface of the casserole with a spoon just before serving.

HELEN FRASER, AVELAND SCHOOL, SLEAFORD, LINCOLNSHIRE

WELSH LAMB CRUMBLE

350 g (12 oz) cooked roast
   Welsh lamb
1 medium onion, peeled
125 g (4 oz) flour
15 ml (1 level tbs) tomato puree

300 ml (½ pt) beef stock
50 g (2 oz) butter
50 g (2 oz) Caerphilly cheese,
   grated
15 ml (1 tbs) mixed herbs

HEAT THE OVEN to 190°C (375°F) Gas Mark 5. Mince together meat and onion. Mix in 15 g ($\frac{1}{2}$ oz) flour, tomato puree, stock and seasoning. Turn into a shallow ovenproof dish. In a bowl, rub the butter into remaining flour until it resembles fine breadcrumbs, then stir in grated cheese, herbs and seasoning. Spoon the crumble over the meat. Bake in the oven for 45 minutes to 1 hour. Serve immediately.

RACHEL DAVIES, PEMBROKE COMPREHENSIVE SCHOOL, BUSH, PEMBROKESHIRE

•

CHESHIRE CUTLETS

4 lamb cutlets
30 ml (2 tbs) fresh wholemeal
   breadcrumbs
30 ml (2 tbs) Cheshire cheese,
   grated
4 small onions, peeled and
   sliced

300 ml ($\frac{1}{2}$ pt) milk
50 g (2 oz) English butter
25 g (1 oz) plain flour
30 ml (2 tbs) fresh single cream
salt and freshly ground pepper,
   to taste

WASH AND DRY cutlets. Grill in ovenproof dish for a few minutes on each side until just browned and sealed. Mix together cheese, breadcrumbs and seasoning and sprinkle over cutlets. Continue to grill cutlets until they are thoroughly cooked. Boil onions in milk until soft. Melt the butter, stir in the flour, cook for a minute or two, then gradually stir in the onions and milk until hot. Add cream but do not boil. Season to taste then pour sauce over cutlets and serve hot.

SARAH AYLOTT, SHAVINGTON HIGH SCHOOL, CREWE, CHESHIRE

LIVER VALENCE

450 g (1 lb) lamb's liver
30 ml (2 tbs) plain flour
225 g (8 oz) onions, peeled and
  thinly sliced
75 g (3 oz) English butter
450 g (1 lb) tomatoes, peeled
  quartered and seeded

15 ml (1 tbs) fresh sage,
  chopped
142 ml (5 fl oz) soured cream
salt and freshly ground black
  pepper, to taste

THINLY SLICE THE lamb's liver into strips. Toss in seasoned flour. In a frying pan lightly brown the onions in butter. Add the tomatoes, cook gently for 5 minutes until soft, and push to the side of the pan. Add the liver and cook over a high heat for about 3 minutes. Sprinkle over the sage. Reduce the heat and spoon in the stirred soured cream. Stir together all the pan ingredients, adjust seasoning and heat, but do not boil. Serve hot, with plain boiled rice.

FIONA HOWARD, SUTTON VALENCE SCHOOL, MAIDSTONE, KENT

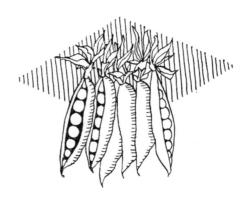

ROAST RABBIT IN CIDER

1 rabbit, skinned and cleaned
450 g (1 lb) parsnips
30 ml (2 tbs) rapeseed oil
4 slices streaky bacon, without
  rind
15 ml (1 tbs) flour

Marinade
300 ml ($\frac{1}{2}$ pt) cider
bunch of fresh herbs (bay leaf,
  thyme, parsley, sage)
2.5 ml ($\frac{1}{2}$ tsp) salt
2.5 ml ($\frac{1}{2}$ tsp) pepper

MARINATE THE RABBIT in cider marinade for 8–12 hours, turning every few hours. Preheat oven to 220°C (425°F) Gas Mark 7. Peel parsnips and cook in boiling water for 5 minutes. Drain, reserving water. Put 15 ml (1 tbs) of oil in the pan to coat parsnips. Remove rabbit from the marinade, reserving liquid. Pat dry and brush with remaining oil. Lay bacon slices over rabbit. Place in roasting tin in preheated oven for 20 minutes. Add parsnips and reduce heat to 180°C (350°F) Gas Mark 4 and continue roasting for a further 1 hour 10 minutes. Take rabbit and parsnips out of oven and place on serving dish. Cover and keep warm. Mix flour with juices in pan and cook for 1 minute. Add reserved marinade and parsnip water gradually stirring to make gravy. Boil, then simmer for 3 minutes. Adjust seasoning.

VICTORIA SOUTHERN, STOURPORT-ON-SEVERN HIGH SCHOOL, WORCESTERSHIRE

PIGEON BREASTS IN GRAVY

4 wood pigeons
120 ml (4 fl oz) red wine
30 ml (2 tbs) rapeseed oil
1 small onion, finely chopped
25 g (1 oz) butter
1 large leek
2 medium carrots
2 sticks of celery

50 g (2 oz) smoked bacon
1 bay leaf
1 garlic clove, crushed
1.75 litres (3 pt) water
5 ml (1 tsp) redcurrant jelly
salt and freshly ground black
  pepper, to taste

REMOVE BREASTS FROM the pigeon carcasses. Mix together wine, oil, onion and pepper and marinate the breasts. Cover and leave in a cool place for 6–8 hours, turning occasionally. Brown the pigeon carcasses in butter in a large saucepan. Add the vegetables, bacon, bay leaf, and garlic. Cook and stir until vegetables begin to colour. Add the water, bring to the boil and then simmer for about $1\frac{1}{2}$ hours to make a good stock. Strain the stock into a saucepan, remove the breasts from the marinade and add the marinade to the pan. Boil rapidly to reduce to a good gravy consistency. Wipe pigeon breasts. Heat a heavy pan until very hot. Sprinkle surface with a little salt, put in breasts and cook for a minute each side to brown, turning three times. Do not cook too long. After about three minutes each side they should be ready. Do not overcook or they will be tough. Slice thickly and serve hot with the gravy.

LISA PICKERING, WEST KIRBY GRAMMAR SCHOOL, WIRRAL, MERSEYSIDE

•

Chef's choice

From the top: Mushroom and Cheshire scallops; Pork with apple and cider sauce accompanied by Garlic roast potatoes and Carrots with lemon and mint; Broccoli mimosa; Bideford pears. Photograph sponsored by the Mushroom Grower's Association.

TROUT WITH WATERCRESS SAUCE

2 bunches watercress, washed
and trimmed
5 ml (1 tsp) lemon juice
5 ml (1 tsp) grated lemon rind
4 × 100 g (3½ oz) fillets rainbow
trout

120 ml (4 fl oz) dry white wine
5 ml (1 tsp) made mustard
150 ml (5 fl oz) fresh soured
cream

PREHEAT THE OVEN to 180°C (350°F) Gas Mark 4. Reserve a few sprigs of watercress for decoration. Place remainder in a pan with the lemon juice, rind and 15 ml (1 tbs) of water. Cook for a few minutes until the watercress is wilted and soft. Place the fish in an ovenproof dish in a single layer, pour over the wine. Cover with foil and bake in the oven for about 30 minutes or until the fish is cooked. Drain liquid from the fish and keep fillets warm. Puree the cooked watercress with the mustard and cream in a processor or blender. Add the cooking liquid from the fish, pour into a pan and heat gently for a few minutes, do not allow to boil. Pour over the trout, and garnish with reserved watercress. Serve with new potatoes and broccoli.

The watercress sauce provides a good source of Vitamin A, C and calcium, as well as iron, Vitamin E and fibre, thus making a very nutritious and healthy accompaniment to any meal – as well as tasting good.

JULIA KEMP, TONBRIDGE GRAMMAR SCHOOL FOR GIRLS, TONBRIDGE, KENT

A fresh taste of Scotland

Smokie pate with oatcakes; Angus beef and venison pie served with Brussels sprouts; Tayberry fool. Photograph sponsored by Golden Fields Pure Rapeseed Oil.

HAZELNUT TROUT

50 g (2 oz) butter
25 g (1 oz) wholemeal
   breadcrumbs
25 g (1 oz) chopped hazelnuts
4 medium-sized trout, cleaned
   and gutted

small bunch of chives
120 ml (4 fl oz) single cream
salt and pepper, to taste

MELT 25 g (1 oz) of the butter, stir in breadcrumbs and hazelnuts, and cook stirring all the time until breadcrumbs have browned. Remove from the heat and put to one side. Place the prepared trout side-by-side in a greased grill pan. Chop the chives and sprinkle over the fish. Dot with the remaining butter and sprinkle with seasoning to taste. Grill for 8–10 minutes or until fish flakes. Heat the cream until warm. Pour over the trout and sprinkle with the hazelnut mixture.

LYNNE REES, ST MARTIN'S SCHOOL, HUTTON, ESSEX

•

GRILLED HERRING AND GOOSEBERRY SAUCE

4 herrings, gutted and with
   heads removed
salt and pepper, to taste

5 ml (1 tsp) sugar
small pinch of ground ginger
watercress sprigs, to garnish

Sauce
225 g (8 oz) gooseberries

P REHEAT GRILL. SEASON herrings with salt and pepper. Place under medium grill for 5 minutes on each side or until cooked. Meanwhile make the sauce. Wash gooseberries and heat without any more water in a saucepan with a tightly fitting lid on a low heat for 10–15 minutes until soft. Puree in a blender, adding sugar and ginger. Serve with the grilled herrings.

Herring is widely caught off the shores of Britain. The tart flavour of the gooseberry sauce in this dish offsets the oiliness of the herrings.

MARGARET WILLSHAW, SIR ROGER MANWOOD'S SCHOOL, SANDWICH, KENT

•

FISH COBBLER

Scone mix
75 g (3 oz) wholemeal flour
40 g (1½ oz) butter
2.5 ml (½ tsp) baking power
30–45 ml (2–3 tbs) milk
salt and pepper, to taste

Filling
450 g (1 lb) cod fillet, skinned
15 g (½ oz) English butter

45 ml (3 tbs) milk
salt and pepper, to taste

Egg sauce
2 eggs
25 g (1 oz) English butter
25 g (1 oz) plain flour
150 ml (¼ pt) milk
salt and pepper, to taste

P REHEAT THE OVEN to 180°C (350°F) Gas Mark 4. Place cod, seasoning and butter in ovenproof dish, cover with foil. Cook for 20–25 minutes. Hard boil the eggs. Crack and place in cold water, shell when cool. To make the scone mix, sieve flour into bowl, rub in butter until mixture resembles fine breadcrumbs. Add salt and baking powder and sufficient milk to make a soft dough. Roll out lightly and using a 3½ cm (1½ in) cutter, cut in circles and brush with milk. Make a roux for the sauce, melting butter in saucepan, adding flour, and cook gently. Strain liquid from fish and add to the sauce stirring con-

tinuously, adding milk as required until sauce is thick and smooth. Chop hard-boiled eggs roughly. Flake fish, removing any bones. Combine sauce with fish and egg and arrange scones on top. Bake in oven for 20 minutes, until scones are cooked and browned on top.

SARAH COLE, MOULSHAM HIGH SCHOOL, CHELMSFORD, ESSEX

•

NORFOLK FISH PIE

225 g (8 oz) carrots, sliced
225 g (8 oz) leeks, sliced
1 celery stick, sliced
450 g (1 lb) potatoes, diced
675 g (1½ lb) white fish, skinned and filleted
450 ml (¾ pt) milk and water
25 g (1 oz) English butter

25 g (1 oz) flour, half wholemeal, half plain
5 ml (1 tsp) mustard powder
45 ml (3 tbs) bran flakes
salt and cayenne pepper, to taste

P REHEAT THE OVEN to 190°C (375°F) Gas Mark 5. Put prepared carrots, leeks and celery into saucepan with water and boil for 10 minutes. Drain and leave aside. Cook potatoes. In another pan simmer fish, milk and water for 10 minutes. Strain fish, reserving liquid.

Make a sauce by melting the butter in a saucepan with the flour and mustard powder. Cook, stirring for 1 minute, then add the reserved fish juices and milk. Cook, stirring, for 3 minutes and season to taste. Add vegetables and flaked fish and transfer to an ovenproof casserole dish.

Mash the potatoes. Add a little milk, mix and beat well. Pile potato on top of fish mixture sprinkling crushed bran flakes on top. Place in the oven for 15 minutes until browned.

SALLY WELDON, ST BERNARD'S HIGH SCHOOL, WESTCLIFF-ON-SEA, ESSEX

STRABANE VEGETABLE PIE

125 g (4 oz) N Ireland Cheddar
  cheese
1 kg (2¼ lb) potatoes, peeled
1 onion, peeled
30 ml (2 tbs) rapeseed oil
3 leeks, finely chopped
450 g (1 lb) carrots, diced
225 g (8 oz) mushrooms, sliced
1 small cauliflower, broken into
  florets

30 ml (2 tbs) fresh parsley
salt and freshly ground black
  pepper, to taste

Topping
125 g (4 oz) N Ireland Cheddar
  cheese

PREHEAT OVEN TO 180°C (350°F) Gas Mark 4. Grate cheese, raw potatoes and half the onion. Mix in 30 ml (2 tbs) of oil and season well. Press mixture into deep 23 cm (9 in) greased pie-dish, building up the sides to form a shell. Bake in the oven for 45 minutes. Meanwhile prepare the vegetables. Heat a little oil and fry remaining sliced half onion, leek, carrots, mushrooms and cauliflower florets slowly for 5–10 minutes. Add parsley, salt and pepper and continue cooking until tender. Pile the vegetables into the baked cheese and potato crust. Sprinkle with grated cheese, heat until the edges of the pie look crispy and the cheese has melted.

SHELLEY SHARMA, STRABANE HIGH SCHOOL, STRABANE, COUNTY TYRONE

SPINACH ROULADE

450 g (1 lb) fresh spinach,
  washed
4 eggs, separated
pinch of nutmeg
30 ml (2 tbs) rapeseed oil
1 onion, chopped
175 g (6 oz) button mushrooms

15 ml (1 tbs) plain flour
150 ml ($\frac{1}{4}$ pt) milk
grated mace
15 ml (1 tbs) grated English
  cheese
salt and pepper, to taste

PREHEAT THE OVEN to 200°C (400°F) Gas Mark 6. Cook the spinach for 5 minutes in a large pan with just the water clinging to the leaves after washing. Drain thoroughly and chop finely. Place in a bowl with the egg yolks, salt, pepper and nutmeg to taste. Mix well. Whisk egg whites until stiff and fold into mixture. Spread mixture evenly in a lined greased 30 × 20 cm (12 × 8 in) swiss roll tin. Cook in the oven for 10–15 minutes until firm and risen. Heat the oil in a pan, add onion and fry until soft. Add the sliced mushrooms for 2–3 minutes. Stir in the flour, then gradually add milk. Add salt and pepper and a little mace to taste, simmer for 2–3 minutes. Sprinkle the cheese on a sheet of greaseproof paper. Turn the roulade out onto the paper and peel off the lining paper. Spread with the filling and roll up. Serve immediately.

SARAH ADKIN, TONBRIDGE GRAMMAR SCHOOL FOR GIRLS, TONBRIDGE, KENT

Vegetables and Salads

~

PARSNIP CROQUETTES

900 g (2 lb) parsnips, peeled
  and sliced
50 g (2 oz) softened butter
30 ml (2 tbs) fresh chopped
  herbs (eg, parsley, chervil,
  tarragon)

5 ml (1 tsp) grated nutmeg
plain flour, for coating
1 egg, beaten
fresh breadcrumbs
salt and freshly ground black
  pepper, to taste

COOK THE PARSNIPS in boiling salted water for 15 to 20 minutes until tender. Drain thoroughly then mash and pass through a sieve or food mill until very smooth. Beat in the butter, herbs, nutmeg and pepper to taste. Leave the mixture to cool slightly, then shape into croquettes 6 × 2.5 cm (2½ × 1 in). Roll the croquettes in flour, then mix in beaten egg and breadcrumbs. Chill in the refrigerator for 1 hour. Heat a deep fat fryer to 180°C (350°F) and deep fry the croquettes for 3–4 minutes. Serve immediately.

An interesting and different way of serving parsnips. The crisp texture and creamy filling make it particularly suitable for serving with casseroles and stews.

LORRAINE SHIMMIN, WEST KIRBY GRAMMAR SCHOOL FOR GIRLS, WIRRAL, MERSEYSIDE

ZESTY CARROTS

675 g (1½ lb) small carrots
finely grated skin of one apple
15 ml (1 tbs) apple juice
25 g (1 oz) English butter

5 ml (1 tsp) light brown sugar
30 ml (2 tbs) cold water
salt and pepper, to taste
chopped parsley, to garnish

SLICE THE CARROTS thickly and put into a saucepan with the apple skin and juice, butter, sugar, water, salt and pepper. Bring to the boil over a high heat and then turn down to simmer. Cover with a tight fitting lid. Simmer for 40 minutes stirring occasionally until the liquid has been reduced to a glaze. Turn the carrots into a warm dish and garnish with chopped parsley.

ANTOINETTE COLEMAN, CHRIST'S HOSPITAL, HORSHAM, WEST SUSSEX

•

LAYERED ONIONS AND POTATOES

800 g (1¾ lb) potatoes, sliced
1 onion, sliced
pinch of grated nutmeg
30 ml (2 tbs) fresh parsley,
  chopped

150 ml (¼ pt) vegetable stock
salt and pepper, to taste

PREHEAT THE OVEN to 190°C (375°F) Gas Mark 5. Lightly grease a shallow dish. Layer with potatoes and onion slices, seasoning the layers with nutmeg, salt, pepper and half the parsley. Finish with a neat layer of potatoes. Pour over the vegetable stock. Cover with aluminium foil and bake for 1 hour (remove foil and cook for further half hour.) Serve hot, garnished with remaining parsley.

GILLIAN McDEVITTE, BELFAST ROYAL ACADEMY, BELFAST, COUNTY ANTRIM

BRUSSELS SPROUTS WITH HAZELNUT BUTTER

450 g (1 lb) small Brussels
  sprouts
1 onion, sliced
50 g (2 oz) butter

50 g (2 oz) hazelnuts, finely
  chopped
large pinch of ground cumin
salt and pepper, to taste

TRIM SPROUTS. MELT butter in a pan and saute the onion until soft, about 5 minutes. Stir in hazelnuts, salt, pepper and cumin. Meanwhile, cook Brussels sprouts in boiling salted water for 8–10 minutes, until just tender. Pour butter and onion mixture over Brussels sprouts and toss over high heat for a few minutes.

SAMANTHA LORD, CHALLNEY GIRLS' HIGH SCHOOL, LUTON, BEDFORDSHIRE

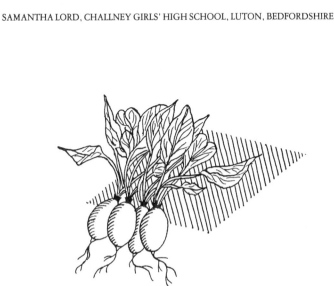

SCALLOPED POTATOES

450 g (1 lb) potatoes
25 g (1 oz) English butter, diced
150 ml ($\frac{1}{4}$ pt) milk

25 g (1 oz) grated cheese
salt and pepper, to taste
chopped parsley, to garnish

PREHEAT OVEN TO 190°C (375°F) Gas Mark 5. Grease an ovenproof casserole dish. Scrub and thinly slice potatoes. Place potatoes in layers in the casserole, season with salt and pepper. Bring milk to boil, pour over the potatoes. Sprinkle with grated cheese, dot with butter. Cook for 30–45 minutes, until brown on top. Sprinkle over the parsley.

SANDRA BROWN, GREENSWARD SCHOOL, HOCKLEY, ESSEX

•

VEGETARIAN SUNBURST SALAD

2 medium carrots
1 large lettuce
$\frac{1}{2}$ cucumber
225 g (8 oz) Cheddar cheese

15 ml (1 heaped tbs) peanut
   butter
30 ml (2 tbs) oil and vinegar
   dressing

WASH, PEEL AND grate the carrots coarsely. Wash and drain the lettuce. Wipe the cucumber and slice thinly. Grate the cheese. Beat peanut butter into dressing, which will become quite thick. Line a salad bowl with lettuce leaves. Arrange the cheese and carrots in alternate heaps around the bowl, divided by cucumber slices, so that each person may take a serving of carrot and cheese with some lettuce. After serving, pour the dressing over each portion.

LESLEY MANTZ, EASTHOLM SCHOOL, PETERBOROUGH, CAMBRIDGESHIRE

WINTER SALAD

1 dessert apple, cored and
   chopped
1 head of celery, sliced
175 g (6 oz) carrot, grated
175 g (6 oz) mushrooms, sliced
1 punet mustard and cress,
   trimmed

2.5 ml ($\frac{1}{2}$ tsp) mustard
2.5 ml ($\frac{1}{2}$ tsp) sugar
60 ml (4 tbs) fresh single cream
10 ml (2 tsp) white wine vinegar
3 hard-boiled eggs, cut in
   wedges
salt and pepper, to taste

LIGHTLY MIX THE apple, celery, carrots and mushrooms together with the cress in a large salad bowl.

To make the dressing, whisk the mustard, sugar, cream and vinegar together. Season to taste. Pour over the salad and toss together. Decorate with hard-boiled eggs. Serve immediately.

HAYLEY JONES, LORD DIGBY'S SCHOOL, SHERBORNE, DORSET

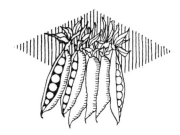

For additional vegetable recipes see the separate Menu section

Hot and Cold Desserts

~

APPLE BETTY

125 g (4 oz) butter
125 g (4 oz) fresh white
  breadcrumbs
125 g (4 oz) soft brown sugar
2.5 ml ($\frac{1}{2}$ level tsp) ground
  cinnamon
grated rind and juice of 1
  lemon

900 g (2 lb) Bramley cooking
  apples, peeled, cored and
  sliced
45 ml (3 tbs) water
cream, to serve

HEAT THE OVEN to 190°C (375°F) Gas Mark 5. Melt the
butter in a saucepan. Remove from heat and mix in the
breadcrumbs. In a bowl mix the sugar, cinnamon and grated
lemon rind. Add the apple slices, and toss in sugar until
coated. Butter a 1.2 litres (2 pt) pie dish. Sprinkle some of the
breadcrumbs in the dish, layer the apple slices alternately with
the crumb mixture, finishing with a layer of crumb mixture.
Mix the lemon juice with the water and spoon over the
pudding. Cover with buttered foil and bake for approximately
30 minutes until apples are cooked, and the topping is crisp
and golden. Serve with single or double cream.

KIRSTY GILHAM, GREENSWARD SCHOOL, HOCKLEY, ESSEX

GOOSEBERRY AND APPLE AMBER

225 g (8 oz) gooseberries,
  topped and tailed
225 g (8 oz) Bramley cooking
  apples, peeled, cored and
  sliced
15 ml (1 tbs) water
25 g (1 oz) butter

25–50 g (1–2 oz) sugar, to taste
15 g ($\frac{1}{2}$ oz) breadcrumbs
2 eggs, separated
1.25 ml ($\frac{1}{4}$ tsp) ground cloves
125 g (4 oz) caster sugar

HEAT THE OVEN to 180°C (350°F) Gas Mark 4. Put the gooseberries, apples, water and butter in a heavy based pan. Cover and cook over a moderate heat for about 10 minutes until tender. Remove from the heat and beat in the sugar, breadcrumbs, egg yolks and cloves. Turn the mixture into four 150 ml ($\frac{1}{4}$ pt) greased ramekins and smooth the surface level. Stand the dishes on a baking sheet and bake in the oven for about 15 minutes until just set. Meanwhile in a clean dry bowl whisk the egg whites until standing in stiff peaks. Fold in the caster sugar, 15 ml (1 tbs) at a time. Whisk until the meringue is stiff and glossy. Swirl or pipe the meringue over the fruit mixture in the ramekins. Lower the oven heat to 140°C (275°F) Gas Mark 1 and return the ramekins to the oven for about 30 minutes, until the meringue is crisp on the outside and lightly browned. Serve hot or cold.

SUSANNAH FARR, ELLERSLIE SCHOOL, MALVERN, WORCESTERSHIRE

SWEET INVICTA

175 g (6 oz) self-raising flour
2 eggs
125 g (4 oz) caster sugar
75 g (3 oz) blackcurrants
75 g (3 oz) raspberries

75 g (3 oz) English Conference
  pears
125 g (4 oz) butter, melted
150 ml (¼ pt) whipping cream
brown sugar

SET THE OVEN at 200°C (400°F) Gas Mark 6. Grease four individual flan tins with melted butter, flour the tins lightly. Sieve the flour. Whisk the eggs and caster sugar until thick, add melted butter. Gently fold in the flour with a metal spoon. Pour mixture into the 4 flan tins. Bake in the middle of the oven for about 10–15 minutes until firm and golden brown. Leave in tins for a few minutes and then turn on to a wire tray to cool. Stew fruit in a pan until the juices run. Drain off juice into a separate bowl. Leave to cool. When both flans and fruit are cold, pour juice over flans to moisten and place stewed fruit on top. Prepare whipping cream and pipe onto sweet. Sprinkle a little brown sugar on top.

NATASHA WYETH, INVICTA GRAMMAR SCHOOL FOR GIRLS, MAIDSTONE, KENT

•

ULSTER CHEESECAKE

Topping
350 g (12 oz) N Ireland Cheddar
  cheese, grated
3 eggs, separated
finely grated rind of 1 lemon
75 g (3 oz) light brown sugar
60 ml (4 tbs) plain yogurt
300 g (11 oz) strawberries

Base
50 g (2 oz) N Ireland butter
25 g (1 oz) medium oatmeal
7.5 ml (1½ tsp) ground ginger
25 g (1 oz) light brown sugar
75 g (3 oz) plain wholemeal
  flour

PREHEAT THE OVEN to 180°C (350°F) Gas Mark 4. To make the base, melt the butter in a saucepan and stir in oatmeal, flour, sugar and ginger. Cook gently for 1–2 minutes, stirring all the time. Spoon into a cake tin with a loose bottom and spread over base. Beat egg yolks, lemon rind and sugar until thick. Whisk egg whites until stiff. Fold yogurt, grated cheese and egg whites into sugar and egg yolk mixture. Pour over base and bake in the oven for 45 minutes. Leave to cool, remove from the tin and decorate with sliced strawberries.

This is a high protein dish that can be eaten by lacto-ovo vegetarians as it contains no gelatine.

LORNA CAMPBELL, BELFAST ROYAL ACADEMY, BELFAST, COUNTY ANTRIM

PEAR PUDDING

675 g (1½ lb) Conference pears
75 g (3 oz) soft brown sugar
zest and juice of 1 orange

Topping
125 g (4 oz) butter

125 g (4 oz) demerara sugar
225 g (8 oz) digestive biscuits
5 ml (1 heaped tsp) cinnamon
175–250 ml (6–8 oz) plain
yogurt

PREHEAT THE OVEN to 180°C(350°F) Gas Mark 4. Peel the pears and cut in half. Put the pears, orange juice and zest, and soft brown sugar in an ovenproof dish and bake, covered for about half an hour or until soft. Let them cool.

Put the digestive biscuits into a plastic bag and with a rolling pin crush them to form crumbs. Melt butter in a saucepan, stir in the crumbs, sugar and cinnamon, and let it cook gently for five minutes, giving the pan an occasional stir. Cover the cooked and cooled pears with the crumb mixture and bake for 15 minutes at 200°C (400°F) Gas Mark 6. Serve with yogurt.

NICHOLAS DE LUCY, SUTTON VALENCE SCHOOL, MAIDSTONE, KENT

AUTUMN PUDDING

675 g (1½ lb) apples and
blackberries
approximately 50 g (2 oz) caster

sugar or to taste
6–8 slices of bread with crusts
removed

LIGHTLY STEW THE fruit (reserving 75 g (3 oz) black-berries) with a little water. Sweeten to taste. Let the fruit cool. Meanwhile arrange the bread, lining the sides and bottom of a 600 ml (1 pt) pudding basin, saving some bread for the top.

When the fruit is cool, strain it and reserve the juice. Add the remaining whole blackberries and mix in. Moisten the bread lining with the reserved juice and transfer the fruit mixture to the bowl. Top with the remaining slices of bread, pressing the fruit down firmly. Cover the bowl with a plate and chill in the fridge for a few hours.

To serve, loosen the pudding around the edges with a knife and turn onto a plate. Serve with cream.

An adaptation of an old recipe for Autumn Pudding, using blackberries and apples. Picking blackberries from the hedgerows will keep down the cost of the dish, and using wholemeal bread will increase its fibre content.

KAREN WADE, ARTHUR MELLOWS VILLAGE COLLEGE, PETERBOROUGH, CAMBRIDGESHIRE

A fresh taste of the Midlands

Shropshire pea soup; Chicken in celery sauce served with Duchesse potatoes and Glazed carrots; Honeyed apple cheesecake. Photograph sponsored by Quality British Chicken.

SPICED APPLE WHIP

450 g (1 lb) Bramley cooking
  apples
1 clove
5 ml (1 tsp) mixed spice
2.5 ml (½ tsp) finely grated
  lemon rind
45 ml (3 tbs) cold water

40 g (1½ oz) sugar
10 ml (2 tsp) gelatine
60 ml (4 tbs) hot water
60 ml (4 tbs) double cream
10 ml (2 tsp) milk
whipped cream and finely
  grated chocolate, to decorate

P EEL, CORE AND roughly chop the apples. Put into sauce-pan with the clove, spice, lemon rind and cold water. Bring slowly to the boil. Reduce heat and simmer covered for 5–10 minutes until fruit is soft. Remove from heat and take out clove. Sweeten to taste with sugar. The Bramleys should have cooked to a thick sauce consistency. Mash with a fork to remove any remaining lumps, or liquidize.

Sprinkle gelatine onto the hot water in a basin over a pan of boiling water. Stir until dissolved. Add to the apple mixture and leave in a cold place until just beginning to thicken and set. Mix the cream and milk together and whisk until lightly stiff. Fold in the fruit mixture. Pour into individual ramekins and leave in fridge to set.

Decorate with piped whipped cream and finely grated chocolate.

VICKY KRALISE, MATTHEW HUMBERSTONE COMPREHENSIVE SCHOOL, CLEETHORPES,
SOUTH HUMBERSIDE

•

A fresh taste of the Southeast

Cream of corn soup; Chicken and apple parcels accompanied by Calabrese with toasted almonds; Kentish potatoes; Raspberry cheesecake. Photograph jointly sponsored by the Milk Marketing Board and the National Dairy Council.

BLACKBERRY AND APPLE MERINGUE BASKET

Meringue

2 egg whites

125 g (4 oz) caster sugar

2.5 ml (½ tsp) vanilla essence

2.5 ml (½ tsp) vinegar

5 ml (1 tsp) cornflour

Filling

275 g (10 oz) Cox's Orange
  Pippin apples

275 g (10 oz) blackberries

125 g (4 oz) sugar

300 ml (½ pt) water

15 ml (1 tbs) cornflour

400 g (14 oz) thick plain yogurt

PREHEAT OVEN TO 150°C (300°F) Gas Mark 2. Beat egg whites until very stiff. Beat in caster sugar gradually, until meringue is shiny and stands in firm peaks. Gently fold in vanilla essence, vinegar and the teaspoon of cornflour. Spread meringue in a 23 cm (9 in) circular tin, lined with cooking parchment, smoothing it out evenly. Bake in centre of the oven for about 1 hour or until firm. Leave to cool then carefully remove the paper. Place on serving plate.

To prepare the filling

Peel, core and slice the apples. Wash and pick over the blackberries. Place sugar and water in a saucepan and stir over low heat until sugar has dissolved. Bring to the boil and simmer for 1 minute. Add the apples to the syrup in the saucepan, simmer gently for 1 minute then add blackberries. Bring back to boil and remove from heat. Leave pan for about 15 minutes with lid on. With slotted spoon carefully lift out fruit from the syrup and put aside. Return syrup to heat and pour in the cornflour, blended with cold water, gradually stirring, until slightly thickened. Cook sauce gently for 2 minutes. Cool.

To assemble

Place drained yogurt on meringue base and arrange the apple and blackberries attractively on top. Spoon on the sauce.

If desired, some of the yogurt may be replaced by whipped cream for a richer pudding.

MARGARET WILLSHAW, SIR ROGER MANWOOD'S SCHOOL, SANDWICH, KENT

•

FRUIT CRISP

450 g (1 lb) Bramley cooking apples
10 ml (2 tsp) clear English honey
30 ml (2 tbs) hot water

50 g (2 oz) jumbo oats
50 g (2 oz) soft brown sugar
15 ml (1 tbs) rapeseed oil
pinch ginger
pinch salt

Topping
50 g (2 oz) pinhead oatmeal

PREHEAT THE OVEN to 180°C (350°F) Gas Mark 4. Peel and slice apples into lemon water, made by adding 5 ml (1 tsp) lemon juice to 600 ml (1 pt) water. Make topping by mixing all the ingredients together. Gently heat honey and water together in a pan. Drain and arrange apples in 4 individual greased ovenproof dishes. Pour on honey and water mixture. Place topping round edge of dishes, leaving centre with fruit on view. Bake in the oven for 20 minutes.

Other fruit in season can be used (eg, blackcurrants, raspberries, gooseberries). Serve with yogurt.

MARY BURROUGH, COCKERMOUTH SCHOOL, COCKERMOUTH, CUMBRIA

Menus for Special Occasions

CHEF'S CHOICE

~

This menu was specially selected from recipes entered in the competition by Philip Corrick, Executive Chef of The Westbury, Mayfair, London, and Trusthouse Forte 'Chef of the Year'.

•

MUSHROOM AND CHESHIRE SCALLOPS

PORK WITH APPLE AND CIDER SAUCE

GARLIC ROAST POTATOES
BROCCOLI MIMOSA
CARROTS WITH LEMON AND MINT

BIDEFORDPEARS
WITH DEVONSHIRE CLOTTED CREAM

MUSHROOM AND CHESHIRE SCALLOPS

65 g (2½ oz) English butter
225 g (8 oz) mushrooms
1 green pepper
1 garlic clove
25 g (1 oz) flour
300 ml (½ pt) milk
50 g (2 oz) Farmhouse Cheshire cheese
15 ml (1 tbs) fresh single cream
salt and freshly ground pepper, to taste
fresh parsley, to garnish
4 scallop shells, to serve

PREHEAT THE OVEN to 190°C (375°F) Gas Mark 5. Melt the butter in a saucepan and lightly fry the mushrooms, pepper and garlic. Divide the mixture between 4 scallop shells. Put the flour and milk into the saucepan and stir over low heat. Add seasoning, half the cheese and the fresh cream. Pour sauce over the mushroom mixture and add the remaining cheese to the top. Bake in the oven for 15 minutes until golden brown. Serve hot, garnished with parsley.

Cheshire is famous for its flaky, creamy cheese and this fresh enticing starter sets the tone for the whole meal. An exciting blend of sliced mushrooms and green peppers covered thickly in a rich Cheshire cheese sauce neatly presented in a whole scallop shell.

SARAH AYLOTT, SHAVINGTON HIGH
SCHOOL, CREWE, CHESHIRE

PORK WITH APPLE AND CIDER SAUCE

575 g (1¼ lb) boned shoulder of pork with rind removed
300 ml (½ pt) cider
1 Bramley cooking apple
extra cider for sauce
15 ml (1 tbs) plain flour
15 ml (1 tbs) rapeseed oil

Stuffing
225 g (½ lb) onions
225 g (½ lb) fresh white breadcrumbs
2.5 ml (½ tsp) sage
2.5 ml (½ tsp) salt
shake of white pepper
pinch of black pepper
25 g (1 oz) melted butter or milk

PLACE PORK IN an ovenproof dish or tray. Pour cider over pork, cover with foil and leave overnight in a cool place, turning several times. Preheat oven to 200°C (400°F) Gas Mark 6.

Prepare stuffing, boil onions in salt water until tender, drain and chop finely. Mix onions with breadcrumbs and add sage, salt, and peppers. Bind with butter or milk until stiff. Remove pork from pan and pat dry. Place stuffing in middle of pork, roll up and secure with string. Return rolled pork to pan with cider used for marinade. Roast pork and cider for about 15 minutes. Remove the pork and pour the cider into a jug. Return pork to the oven and baste with cider at periodic intervals so that it is absorbed by the meat. Roast for about 1½ to 2 hours. Peel and core apple and cut into small chunks and place in a pan with small amount of cider or water. Cook

gently until apple softens, remove from pan and make into a puree. When pork is cooked, place on a serving dish, cover and keep warm. Reserve juices. Heat oil in roasting tin, stir in flour and cook gently for 1 minute, then add reserved juices and extra cider, stirring constantly to make sauce. Adjust seasoning to taste. Serve pork sliced with the apple puree and cider sauce, and a selection of vegetables.

SALLY TIMMIS, STOURPORT-ON-SEVERN
HIGH SCHOOL, WORCESTERSHIRE

•

GARLIC ROAST POTATOES

4 medium-size home grown
  potatoes
1 garlic clove
120 ml (4 fl oz) rapeseed oil

PREHEAT OVEN TO 220°C (425°F) Gas Mark 7. Peel the potatoes and boil in salted water for 3 minutes. Crush garlic and mix to a fine paste with the oil. Remove potatoes from the pan and drain. Cut in slices almost through to base. Coat in garlic and oil and roast in a hot oven for 1 hour, basting with oil occasionally.

LYNSEY TAYLOR, GREENSWARD SCHOOL,
HOCKLEY, ESSEX

BROCCOLI MIMOSA

625 g (1 lb 6 oz) broccoli
3 spring onions or shallots, chopped
90 ml (6 tbs) chicken stock
45 ml (3 tbs) low fat yogurt
1 egg, hard-boiled
30 ml (2 tbs) flaked almonds
salt and pepper, to taste

TRIM THE BROCCOLI so that stems are the same width. Arrange the broccoli pieces in the base of a saucepan in boiling salted water. Cover and simmer for 6–8 minutes. Drain thoroughly and place in a warm serving dish. Put spring onions and stock into sauce-pan to boil. Remove from the heat, stir in the yogurt, return to heat and warm through gently. Season and spoon over the broccoli. Sprinkle finely chopped egg and flaked almonds over the top. Serve immediately.

GILLIAN McDEVITTE, BELFAST ROYAL
ACADEMY, BELFAST, COUNTY ANTRIM

CARROTS WITH LEMON AND MINT

675 g (1½ lb) new carrots, trimmed
  and scrubbed
finely grated rind and juice of half a
  lemon
30 ml (2 tbs) fresh mint, chopped

COOK CARROTS FOR 10 minutes in boiling salted water and drain. Add lemon juice, rind and mint and toss together. Serve immediately.

JAYNE TURNER, NEWCASTLE UNDER LYME
SCHOOL, NORTH STAFFORDSHIRE

BIDEFORD PEARS WITH DEVONSHIRE CLOTTED CREAM

4 large firm Comice pears
25 g (1 oz) blanched almonds
  (halves)
120 ml (8 tbs) redcurrant jelly
150 ml (¼ pt) water
15 ml (1 tbs) caster sugar
2 cloves
½ stick cinnamon
clotted cream

PEEL PEARS, LEAVING stalks on. Spike them with almond halves. Dissolve redcurrant jelly in water in a pan over a low heat. Add sugar, cloves and cinnamon stick, stir until sugar has dissolved. Add pears and simmer gently for about 15 minutes until the pears are tender. Transfer pears to serving dish. Boil the syrup until it is reduced by half. Serve pears hot or cold, with clotted cream.

LYNDA SLEE, EDGEHILL COLLEGE,
BIDEFORD, DEVON

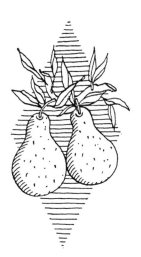

A FRESH TASTE OF SCOTLAND

~

YOU CAN ALMOST hear the skirl of pipes as you read Ailsa Campbell's menu with its use of distinctive Scottish produce. Her fish pate is made from Arbroath smokies; a tasty haddock, slow-smoked over oak chips in sugar bags, the starter is teamed with nutty-flavoured fresh oatcakes. The main course features a handsome pie of Angus beef, venison and parsnips cooked in a rich tomato and beef stock. The fruit fool dessert is made with Tayberries, a cross between blackberries and raspberries developed in Scotland.

•

SMOKIE PATE WITH OATCAKES

ANGUS BEEF AND VENISON PIE WITH PARSNIPS
ROAST POTATOES, BRUSSELS SPROUTS AND CARROTS

TAYBERRY FOOL

AILSA CAMPBELL, ARBROATH HIGH SCHOOL, ARBROATH, TAYSIDE

SMOKIE PATE WITH OATCAKES

1 pair Arbroath smokies
150 g (5 oz) plain cottage cheese
30 ml (2 tbs) yogurt
25 g (1 oz) melted butter
lemon juice
lettuce leaves, watercress and lemon
    wedges, to garnish

Oatcakes
125 g (4 oz) oatmeal
25 g (1 oz) rapeseed oil
pinch salt

To prepare the pate

CUT OPEN AND remove all bones and skin from the smokies. Put flesh into mixing bowl, add cottage cheese, yogurt, and melted butter. Mix together until a soft shaped ball is formed. Press into a round bowl and chill for one hour.

To prepare the oatcakes

Preheat the oven to 180°C (350°F) Gas Mark 4. Put all ingredients into a bowl and mix, adding enough boiling water to form a stiff dough. Knead and roll out on a floured surface. Cut into 4 or 8 circles depending on size required, place on a baking tray and bake until firm to the touch, approximately 15–20 minutes.

To serve

Cut pate into 4 wedges and serve on lettuce leaf on individual plates. Place oatcakes (1 or 2) to the side and garnish with watercress.

Unique to Arbroath, smokies are small haddock, with heads removed, which have been salted for two hours. They are then hung in pairs to be slow-smoked in sugar bags over beech or oak.

ANGUS BEEF AND VENISON PIE WITH PARSNIPS

30 ml (2 tbs) rapeseed oil
350 g (¾ lb) chuck steak, cubed
225 g (½ lb) venison, cubed
1 large onion, sliced and chopped
25 g (1 oz) wholemeal flour
450 g (1 lb) tomatoes, peeled and
    chopped
1 beef stock cube
bunch of fresh herbs (parsley, bay
    leaf, thyme and tarragon)
250 g (9 oz) parsnips, peeled and
    sliced
225 g (8 oz) puff pastry
salt and pepper, to taste
egg or milk, to glaze

PREHEAT OVEN TO 180°C (350°F) Gas Mark 4. Heat 30 ml (2 tbs) of oil in a large frying pan, add meat and onion and fry until well browned. Sprinkle with flour and cook for 1–2 minutes, stirring constantly. Stir in the chopped tomatoes with juice, crumble the stock cube and stir well into mixture. Add fresh herbs and season with salt and pepper. Bring to the boil, stirring, then transfer to pie or casserole dish and cook for a further ¾ hour until meat is tender. Boil parsnips and add to the casserole and cook for a further 15–20 minutes. Roll out the pastry on a lightly floured board to the shape of but slightly larger than, the casserole dish. Cut from this a long narrow strip of pastry all the way round. Remove casserole from oven and discard bay leaf; add more seasoning if required. Increase oven temperature

to 220°C (425°F) Gas Mark 7. Brush rim of casserole dish with water and press long narrow strip of pastry all the way around. Brush the strip of pastry with water and place rest of pastry on top. Press the edges down firmly with fork or thumb and finger to seal them. Make a cross in the middle to let steam escape, folding back pastry to make a square. Brush with beaten egg or milk. Bake for about 20–25 minutes or until pastry is well risen and golden brown. Serve hot.

TAYBERRY FOOL

350 g (12 oz) tayberries
75 g (3 oz) sugar
150 ml (¼ pt) double cream
150 ml (¼ pt) yogurt
30 ml (2 tbs) low fat milk
a few tayberries for decoration

PUREE FRUIT AND sweeten with sugar. Whip double cream, yogurt and milk together until very thick. Gradually fold in fruit puree. Place in four sundae glasses and chill for 2 hours. Decorate with a few whole tayberries.

Tayberries are a cross between a blackberry and a raspberry and are in season during July to mid-August. They freeze well. Scottish tayberries are said to be superior in flavour to any others due to their slow ripening in the cooler summer.

A FRESH TASTE OF NORTHERN IRELAND

~

DELIA DEVLIN'S MENU owes much of its inspiration to her family. With a father who is a fish merchant, she found it natural to include as a main course a tasty Haddock crumble—fresh haddock under breadcrumb topping with cheese, parsley and hazelnuts to give a crunch. The first course salad is her own invention, a healthy raw salad with yogurt dressing—perhaps inspired by her uncle, a mushroom grower, and grandfather, who loves to tend his vegetable patch.

•

DELIA'S COUNTRY SURPRISE

HADDOCK CRUMBLE
GLAZED DERRY CARROTS
BAKED POTATOES AND BRUSSELS SPROUTS

BAKED APPLE CHEESECAKE

DELIA DEVLIN, ST PIUS X HIGH SCHOOL, MAGHERAFELT, COUNTY DERRY

DELIA'S COUNTRY SURPRISE

125 g (4 oz) raw mushrooms
2 celery sticks
½ cucumber
30 ml (2 tbs) chives, finely chopped
2 eggs, hard-boiled
2 tomatoes, peeled and deseeded
4 lettuce leaves
150 g (5 oz) natural yogurt

CHOP INGREDIENTS FINELY and place in a bowl. Shred lettuce and place in bottom of four serving glasses. Mix ingredients with natural yogurt and spoon into dishes. Serve with wholemeal bread.

HADDOCK CRUMBLE

850 g (1 lb 14 oz) haddock fillets
1 small onion
juice of ½ lemon
30 ml (2 tbs) cold water
125 g (4 oz) fresh wholemeal
   breadcrumbs
50 g (2 oz) Cheddar cheese,
   grated
50 g (2 oz) hazelnuts, finely chopped
15 ml (1 tbs) parsley, chopped
25 g (1 oz) butter
salt and freshly ground black
   pepper, to taste

PREHEAT THE OVEN to 180°C (350°F) Gas Mark 4. Skin the fish, wipe the fillets and arrange on a greased ovenproof dish. Peel and chop the onion and sprinkle it over the fish with lemon juice, salt and pepper. Add 30 ml (2 tbs) cold water. Combine the breadcrumbs with the cheese, nuts, parsley, salt and freshly ground black pepper. Melt the butter and stir it into the crumble mixture. Spread evenly over the fish. Bake for 25–30 minutes or until the crumble is golden brown. Serve with vegetables, for example, glazed Derry carrots, Brussels sprouts and baked potatoes.

GLAZED DERRY CARROTS

800 g (1 lb 12 oz) carrots, trimmed
   and scrubbed
50 g (2 oz) N Ireland butter
450 ml (¾ pt) water
salt and pepper, to taste
chopped parsley, to garnish

PUT THE CARROTS in a saucepan with half the butter, salt
and water. Bring to the boil and then
cook for 45 minutes (uncovered)
until the liquid has evaporated. Add
the remaining butter and pepper
and toss the carrots until evenly
glazed. Turn out into a serving dish
and garnish with parsley.

BAKED APPLE CHEESECAKE

125 g (4 oz) N Ireland butter
125 g (4 oz) sugar, light brown
450 g (1 lb) N Ireland cottage cheese
2 eggs, separated
50 g (2 oz) semolina
350 g (12 oz) Bramley cooking
   apples, peeled, poached and
   sweetened to taste
5 ml (1 tsp) icing sugar

PREHEAT THE OVEN to 190°C
(375°F) Gas Mark 5. Cream
together the butter and sugar until
very pale and fluffy. Beat in the
cheese and egg yolks until smooth
and thoroughly combined. Gradually fold in the ground semolina
and the apples. Whisk the egg
whites until stiff but not dry and
gently fold into the mixture with a
metal spoon or spatula. Lightly oil
the base and sides of a deep 20 cm
(8 in) round, loose-based flan tin.
Spoon in the mixture and bake for
about 45–50 minutes, or until
golden brown and just firm to the
touch. Leave to cool in tin for about
1 hour. (The cheesecake will sink
slightly.) Dust with icing sugar and
decorate with sliced apples, dipped
in lemon juice to stop them turning
brown.

A FRESH TASTE OF NORTHERN ENGLAND

~

LAMB AS A main course dish is a choice close to home for Karen Storr, a farmer's daughter from Laversdale in Cumbria. She dreamed up her own special stuffing based on chopped ham and mushrooms with an added tang of rosemary and lemon. Her dessert is a scrumptious fruit pie with a drift of meringue topping the lovely orchard fruits—bramble and apple.

●

LEEK AND POTATO SOUP

LAVERSDALE LAMB
POTATO NESTS FILLED WITH FRESH GARDEN PEAS
JULIENNE CARROTS WITH CHOPPED PARSLEY

BRAMBLE AND APPLE MERINGUE

KAREN STORR, WILLIAM HOWARD UPPER SCHOOL, BRAMPTON, CUMBRIA
CELEBRATION YOUNG COOK OF THE YEAR

LEEK AND POTATO SOUP

450 g (1 lb) leeks, washed well,
  trimmed and sliced
125 g (4 oz) onions, finely chopped
25 g (1 oz) butter
350 g (12 oz) potatoes, peeled and
  chopped into cubes
600 ml (1 pt) chicken stock
300 ml ($\frac{1}{2}$ pt) milk
salt and freshly ground black
  pepper, to taste
swirl of fresh cream and chopped
  chives, to garnish

FRY LEEKS AND onions gently
in the butter, until soft but not
brown, for approximately 8 minutes. Add potatoes, stock, salt and
pepper. Bring to the boil and
simmer for 20–30 minutes until soft.
Liquidise, add milk and reheat
gently. Serve hot with a swirl of fresh
cream and sprinkle with chopped
chives.

*This is a popular dish in Carlisle, after the
Annual Leek Show, and makes a thoroughly
nourishing soup, ideal for a cold winter's day.*

LAVERSDALE LAMB

125 g (4 oz) mushrooms, finely
  chopped
125 g (4 oz) locally produced cooked
  ham, diced
50 g (2 oz) fresh wholemeal
  breadcrumbs
50 g (2 oz) butter
1 egg, beaten
5 ml (1 tsp) grated lemon rind or
5 ml (1 tsp) fresh rosemary, chopped
1.25 kg (2$\frac{1}{2}$ lb) boned shoulder of
  lamb
salt and pepper, to taste

PREHEAT OVEN TO 190°C
(375°F) Gas Mark 5. Fry mushrooms in the butter until soft. Add
ham, breadcrumbs, salt and pepper,
lemon rind or rosemary. Bind with
beaten egg. Spread stuffing on
lamb, roll up and secure with string.
Roast in the oven for about 1$\frac{3}{4}$–2
hours.

*The ingredients in this recipe complement each
other well and make a cheaper cut of lamb look
and taste rather special.*

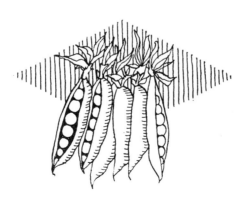

POTATO NESTS WITH FRESH GARDEN PEAS

675 (1½ lb) peeled potatoes
1 egg, beaten
knob of butter
450 g (1 lb) fresh garden peas
salt and freshly ground black
   pepper, to taste

PREHEAT THE OVEN to 190°C (375°F), Gas Mark 5. Cut the potatoes into even-sized pieces and place in salted boiling water and cook for 15 minutes or until soft. Drain, add butter, then beat in the egg until the mixture is light and fluffy. Season with salt and freshly ground black pepper. Pipe into nests on to a greased baking tray. Cook in the oven for about 20 minutes or until lightly browned. Serve hot, the centres filled with cooked fresh garden peas.

~

An interesting way of serving ordinary potatoes; the browing adds colour and crispness and they also freeze well.

•

JULIENNE CARROTS WITH CHOPPED PARSLEY

450 g (1 lb) fresh carrots
25 g (1 oz) English butter
parsley, chopped
4 spring onions, chopped

SCRAPE CARROTS AND slice into 5 cm (2 in) matchsticks.

Cook in salted boiling water for about 10 minutes, or until tender. Drain, toss in butter, place in a serving dish and sprinkle with chopped parsley. Garnish with spring onions.

•

BRAMBLE AND APPLE MERINGUE

175 g (6 oz) short crust pastry
225 g (8 oz) blackberries
225 g (8 oz) Bramley cooking apples, peeled and sliced
200 g (7 oz) sugar
2 eggs, separated

PREHEAT THE OVEN to 190°C (375°F) Gas Mark 5. Line a 18 cm (7 in) flan ring with the short crust pastry and bake blind in the oven for about 20 minutes. Lower oven temperature to 160°C (325°F) Gas Mark 3. Cook blackberries, apples and 75 g (3 oz) sugar gently in a saucepan until soft, approximately 15 minutes. Puree and add egg yolks. Pour blackberry and apple mixture into flan case. Whisk egg whites until stiff, gradually beat in the remaining sugar until egg whites stand in stiff peaks. Pipe on top of filling. Bake in the oven for 20–30 minutes until golden brown.

~

The crispy sweet meringue compliments the sharp taste of the brambles and apples. Picking blackberries from the hedgerows will cut down on the cost of the dish.

A FRESH TASTE OF THE MIDLANDS

~

ELIZABETH CHAMBERS' MENU starts with a warming, minty Shropshire pea soup, served with toasted flapovers, as an interesting change from croutons. Her creamy honey-flavoured cheesecake is topped with glazed slices of English apples.

•

SHROPSHIRE PEA SOUP WITH TOASTED FLAPOVERS

CHICKEN IN CELERY SAUCE

DUCHESSE POTATOES AND GLAZED CARROTS

HONEYED APPLE CHEESECAKE

ELIZABETH CHAMBERS, KING EDWARD VI HIGH SCHOOL FOR GIRLS, BIRMINGHAM

SHROPSHIRE PEA SOUP WITH TOASTED FLAPOVERS

50 g (2 oz) English butter
1 small onion, peeled and finely
    chopped
900 g (2 lb) peas, shelled
1.2 litres (2 pt) chicken stock
2.5 ml ($\frac{1}{2}$ tsp) sugar
2 large sprigs of mint
2 egg yolks
150 ml (5 fl oz) double cream
salt and freshly ground black
    pepper, to taste
sprig of mint, to garnish

Toasted flapovers
8 thin slices of bread, crusts removed
butter

MELT THE BUTTER in a large
saucepan, add onion and cook
for 5 minutes until soft. Add the
peas, stock, sugar and sprigs of mint.
Bring to the boil and cook for about
30 minutes. Put the soup through a
fine sieve or puree in a blender.
Return to pan and add seasoning. In
a bowl, beat together the yolks and
fresh cream and add to the soup.
Heat gently, stirring but do not boil
otherwise it will curdle. Transfer to a
warmed soup tureen and garnish
with a sprig of mint.

To prepare toasted flapovers
Preheat the oven to 200°C (400°F)
Gas Mark 6. Spread bread with
butter. Fold diagonally opposite
corners into the centre, overlapping
and securing with a toothpick.
Brown in the oven on a baking tray.
Serve hot or cold according to taste.

CHICKEN IN CELERY SAUCE

100 g (4 oz) English butter
4 chicken breasts
1 small head of celery, washed and
    diced
25 g (1 oz) flour
450 ml ($\frac{3}{4}$ pt) semi-skimmed milk
$\frac{1}{4}$ cucumber, cut into matchsticks
5 ml (1 tsp) capers
salt and freshly ground black
    pepper, to taste

HEAT 75 g (3 oz) butter in a pan
and gently fry the chicken.
Remove and keep warm. Cook the
celery in salted water until tender
then rub through a sieve or puree in
a blender. Melt the remaining butter
in a pan, stir in the flour and cook
gently for 1 minute, stirring.

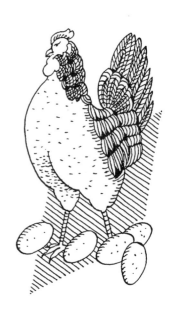

Remove pan from the heat and gradually stir in the milk. Bring to the boil, add the celery, and continue to cook, stirring, for 5 minutes, then add the cucumber, capers and seasoning to taste. Put the chicken on a hot serving dish and pour over the sauce. Serve with duchesse potatoes and glazed carrots.

•

DUCHESSE POTATOES

225 g (8 oz) potatoes
15 ml (1 tbs) margarine
1 egg yolk or ½ beaten egg
15 ml (1 tbs) cream
pepper, salt and nutmeg, to taste

PREHEAT THE OVEN to 200°C (400°F) Gas Mark 6. Boil the potatoes, and then push through a wire sieve. In a saucepan melt the margarine and beat in the potatoes, season. Add the egg and beat until smooth. Add a little cream, if the mixture is dry.
　Put the potato mixture into a forcing bag with a large star pipe, and pipe large rosettes, stars or zig zag finger shapes onto a greased tray. Place in oven and cook until golden brown.

•

HONEYED APPLE CHEESECAKE

Base
50 g (2 oz) digestive biscuits, crushed
25 g (1 oz) English butter, melted
25 g (1 oz) caster sugar

Filling
125 g (4 oz) low fat soft cheese
40 g (1½ oz) caster sugar
60 ml (4 tbs) natural yogurt
5 ml (1 tsp) honey
7 g (¼ oz) gelatine
30 ml (2 tbs) water
120 ml (4 fl oz) whipping cream
25 g (1 oz) kiwi fruit, peeled and chopped

Topping
2 English dessert apples, one red, one green, cored and sliced, but not peeled
30 ml (2 tbs) honey
30 ml (2 tbs) water
hazelnuts, halved

MIX BISCUITS WITH melted butter and stir in the sugar. Press into a 20 cm (8 in) greased loose bottomed cake tin. Leave to set. Cream the cheese and sugar until smooth and gradually add the yogurt and honey. Dissolve gelatine in the water placed in basin over a pan of hot water. Cool and add to the cheese mixture, blending thoroughly. Whisk the cream until thick. Fold into the mixture until well blended. Stir in the kiwi fruit and pour mixture onto the crumb base. Chill until firm. Remove the cheesecake from the tin. Poach the apple slices gently in the honey and water until soft. Cool completely. Decorate the cheesecake with sliced apples and nuts. Brush with more honey. Serve cold.

~

The red and green skins of the apples are most attractive arranged on top of the cheesecake. Leaving the skins on also adds fibre to the dish, as does the digestive biscuit base.

A FRESH TASTE OF THE SOUTHEAST

~

JULIE EDWARDS FOUND plenty of inspiration for her menu from her home county of Kent, so often called 'The Garden of England'. Her Cream of corn soup uses sweetcorn, a crop gaining in popularity throughout the southeast. For her main course she chose chicken breasts wrapped in smoked bacon, with an unusual stuffing of apple slices and served in a sauce based on apple juice.

•

CREAM OF CORN SOUP

CHICKEN AND APPLE PARCELS
SERVED WITH
KENTISH POTATOES
CALABRESE WITH TOASTED ALMONDS

RASPBERRY CHEESECAKE

JULIE EDWARDS, TONBRIDGE GRAMMAR SCHOOL FOR GIRLS, TONBRIDGE, KENT

CREAM OF CORN SOUP

1 medium onion
1 large potato
50 g (2 oz) English butter
750 ml (1¼ pt) chicken stock
300 g (11 oz) sweetcorn kernels
10 ml (2 tsp) cornflour
120 ml (4 fl oz) semi-skimmed milk
salt and cayenne pepper, to taste
chopped parsley and swirl of double
   cream, to garnish

PEEL THE ONION and potato,
cut into pieces and chop finely.
Melt the butter in a pan and cook the
onion and potato gently for 5 minutes. Add the stock, bring to the boil
and then simmer for 15 minutes.
Add the sweetcorn kernels and cook
for 5 minutes. Put the soup into a
blender or processor and blend for 1
minute. Mix the cornflour with a
little of the milk. Add this mixture
and remaining milk to the soup and
blend for 10 seconds. Return to pan
and reheat, stirring well until it
thickens. Season to taste. Serve
decorated with chopped parsley and
a swirl of double cream with melba
toast.

The sweetcorn gives this soup a lovely creamy
colour and it is a good and warming dish for
cold days.

CHICKEN AND APPLE PARCELS

2 English dessert apples
4 large skinless chicken breasts
8 long rashers smoked bacon, rind
   removed
15 ml (1 tbs) rapeseed oil
1 garlic clove, crushed
300 ml (½ pt) English apple juice
5 ml (1 tsp) cornflour
salt and freshly ground black
   pepper, to taste
chopped parsley, to garnish

PEEL, CORE AND slice one
apple. Flatten chicken breasts
with a rolling pin. Place a few slices
of the apple in the centre of each
chicken breast and roll up. Wrap
each one with 2 rashers of bacon and
secure with wooden cocktail sticks to
make 4 neat parcels. Heat the oil
with the garlic in a pan and brown
the parcels on each side for 5 minutes. Peel and core the remaining
apple then cut across to make rings.
Place one on top of each parcel, add
the apple juice and season. Cover
and simmer gently for 15 minutes.
Correct the seasoning to taste.

   Remove the chicken from the
pan to a warm serving dish. Mix the
cornflour with 15 ml (1 tbs) water
and add to the pan juices, stirring
and cook until thickened. Spoon the
sauce over each parcel and serve.
Garnish with chopped parsley.

Chicken and apple parcels look delicate but not
too fussy. Chicken is an ideal meat for a special
meal on a budget, and the bacon adds extra
flavour.

KENTISH POTATOES

1 garlic clove, crushed
675 g (1½ lb) potatoes, peeled and
 thinly sliced
1 onion, thinly sliced
600 ml (1 pt) milk
45 ml (3 tbs) plain flour
15 ml (1 tbs) parsley, finely chopped
50 g (2 oz) mature Cheddar, grated
25 g (1 oz) butter
salt and pepper, to taste

PREHEAT THE OVEN to 190°C
(375°F) Gas Mark 5. Prepare a
1.75 litre (3 pt) casserole dish by
rubbing the crushed garlic around
the bowl. Using the prepared dish,
arrange the potato and onion in
layers, seasoning each layer. Blend
the plain flour with a little milk and
pour the flour mixture and
remaining milk over the potatoes.
Sprinkle with parsley and cheese and
dot with knobs of butter. Cook for
about 1¼ hours, until the potatoes
are cooked and the top is golden
brown.

•

CALABRESE WITH TOASTED ALMONDS

675 g (1½ lb) calabrese or broccoli
25 g (1 oz) English butter
50 g (2 oz) flaked almonds

WASH AND TRIM the
calabrese. Cook in boiling
water for 5–10 minutes, until tender.
Meanwhile, melt butter in a large
frying pan, add the almonds and
heat gently, stirring all the time until

browned. Drain calabrese into
serving dish and sprinkle over the
toasted almonds. A little lemon
juice may be added if desired. Serve
at once.

~

*Calabrese is most commonly known as broccoli.
However, there are regional variations in the use
of the different names. For example, in Lincolnshire spring-maturing cauliflowers are called
broccoli, whereas in Cornwall the winter-
maturing variety is called broccoli. But some
shops throughout the country continue to call
the vegetable calabrese.*

•

RASPBERRY CHEESECAKE

Pastry
50 g (2 oz) English butter
125 g (4 oz) plain flour
10 ml (2 tsp) sugar
pinch salt
1 egg yolk

Topping
225 g (8 oz) cottage cheese
150 ml (¼ pt) double cream
rind and juice of 1 lemon
50 g (2 oz) caster sugar
225 g (½ lb) raspberries

PREHEAT THE OVEN to 200°C
(400°F) Gas Mark 6. Rub butter
into flour until the mixture
resembles fine breadcrumbs, add
sugar and salt, then bind with egg
yolk. Roll out carefully to fit 23 cm
(9 in) fluted flan ring. Bake blind for
20–25 minutes until completely
cooked. Prepare the topping. Rub
cottage cheese through a sieve.
Whip cream until thick. Fold
cheese, rind and juice of lemon, and
sugar gently into cream. Spread over
pastry case and chill well. Decorate
with raspberries and serve.

A FRESH TASTE
OF THE
SOUTHWEST

~

S USAN WOOD'S VERWOOD vegetable pancakes make a delicious main course, particularly suitable for non-meat eaters. The pancakes, stuffed with a mixture of ten different vegetables, are coated with tasty Cheddar cheese sauce and served golden and bubbling from the grill. She finishes off the meal with delectable Devonshire fruit parcels with clotted cream.

•

SUSAN'S STUFFED EGGS

VERWOOD VEGETABLE PANCAKES
WITH CHEDDAR CHEESE SAUCE
CLOVELLY APPLE AND CELERY SALAD

DEVONSHIRE FRUIT PARCELS WITH
CLOTTED CREAM

SUSAN WOOD, EDGEHILL COLLEGE, BIDEFORD, DEVON

SUSAN'S STUFFED EGGS

4 eggs
75 g (3 oz) cream cheese
30 ml (2 tbs) mayonnaise
15 ml (1 tbs) parsley, chopped
lettuce leaves
1 tomato
paprika pepper
salt and pepper, to taste

HARD BOIL AND shell the eggs. Cut in half lengthwise. Spoon out the yolks and mash them in a mixing bowl, with the cream cheese and mayonnaise. Mix well and add seasoning and parsley. Taste and adjust seasoning if needed. Pipe mixture back into egg white cases. Wash lettuce and tomato. Slice tomato and arrange on four plates. Place two half eggs on each plate and sprinkle with paprika pepper.

•

VERWOOD VEGETABLE PANCAKES WITH CHEDDAR CHEESE SAUCE

(8 pancakes)

Batter
125 g (4 oz) plain flour
1.25 ml (¼ tsp) salt
1 egg
250 ml (8 fl oz) milk
rapeseed oil, for frying

Filling
1 small cauliflower, broken into
  florets

75 g (3 oz) broccoli, broken into
  florets
1 potato, diced
1 swede, diced
1 carrot, sliced
1 onion, sliced
1 courgette, sliced
1 parsnip, diced
1 leek, sliced
75 g (3 oz) mushrooms, sliced

Sauce
50 g (2 oz) butter
50 g (2 oz) plain flour
500 ml (18 fl oz) milk
10 ml (2 tsp) salt
125 g (4 oz) mature English Cheddar
  cheese, grated
15 g (½ oz) fresh white breadcrumbs
freshly ground black pepper, to taste
parsley, to garnish

SIEVE FLOUR AND salt into a mixing bowl and make a well in the centre, add the egg. With a wooden spoon stir the egg and draw in the flour from the edges. Gradually add just enough milk to incorporate all the flour and make a thick paste. Beat very well to remove any lumps and to give a smooth mixture. Stir in the remaining milk a little at a time. Beat the batter very thoroughly until small air bubbles appear all over the surface. Leave to stand. Put vegetables into a bowl and mix. Heat oil in frying pan and gently cook vegetables until tender. Heat second frying pan with some oil and pour in small quantity of batter, fry gently on both sides until brown. Turn out on to plate and keep warm. Repeat this process until 8 pancakes have been made. Spoon vegetables onto the pancakes, roll them up and keep warm on an ovenproof serving dish.

To make the sauce

Melt fat in a saucepan over a gentle heat. Add flour and stir for 1–2 minutes using a wooden spoon. Remove pan from heat and gradually add half of the milk, stirring briskly all the time. Stir in remaining milk. Return pan to the heat, stirring well all the time and bring the sauce to boiling point and cook for 1–2 minutes. Remove from heat, add seasoning and cheese to sauce, reserving 10 g ($\frac{1}{2}$ oz) cheese for topping, beat in well until smooth. Keep hot until required.

To serve

Pour cheese sauce over pancakes, top with grated cheese and breadcrumb mix and place under hot grill until cheese is browned and bubbling. Garnish with parsley sprigs. Serve immediately.

•

CLOVELLY APPLE AND CELERY SALAD

450 g (1 lb) English dessert apples
30 ml (2 tbs) lemon juice
5 ml (1 tsp) caster sugar
150 ml ($\frac{1}{4}$ pt) mayonnaise
$\frac{1}{2}$ head of celery, chopped
50 g (2 oz) hazelnuts, halved
1 lettuce, separated into leaves

SLICE ONE APPLE thinly and dice remainder. Dip apple into a little lemon juice. Make the dressing with remaining lemon juice, caster sugar and 15 ml (1 tbs) mayonnaise. Toss diced apple in dressing and leave to stand for 30 minutes. Add celery and hazelnuts to diced apple mixture and mix thoroughly. Line a serving bowl with lettuce leaves, pile salad in centre and garnish with apple slices.

•

DEVONSHIRE FRUIT PARCELS

Shortcrust pastry
200 g (7 oz) plain flour
5 ml (1 tsp) salt
100 g ($3\frac{1}{2}$ oz) English butter
60 ml (4 fl oz) cold water

Filling
2 medium Bramley cooking apples, peeled and cored
2 medium Conference pears, peeled and cored
3 plums, stoned
75 g (3 oz) blackberries
juice of 1 lemon
40 g ($1\frac{1}{2}$ oz) sugar

PREHEAT THE OVEN to 220°C (425°F) Gas Mark 7. Sieve flour and salt into a mixing bowl. Rub in butter until the mixture resembles fine breadcrumbs. Add sufficient cold water to give a firm dough. Knead lightly with fingertips. Turn dough on to a lightly floured board. Roll out pastry to about 3.5 mm ($\frac{1}{8}$ in) in thickness. Cut pastry into 8 squares, 15 cm (6 in) in size. Slice apples, pears, and plums thinly and cut into relatively small pieces. Soak in lemon juice. Cut blackberries in half lengthwise. Mix fruit in a bowl, add sugar. Add even amounts to each square of pastry. Brush the edges of the pastry with milk and fold each corner into the centre to look like an envelope. Glaze with milk. Bake in the oven until lightly browned. Reduce heat to cook filling for a further 10 minutes. Serve with clotted Devon cream.

CELEBRATION LUNCHEON

~

SELECTED TO PLEASE the palates of the Lord Forte of Ripley and the judges at the cookery final of 'A Fresh Taste of Britain', this meal uses foods that are widely available fresh all over the country.

An ususual starter of Stilton and pear flan is followed by Lakeland trout fillets filled with a delicious mixture of mushrooms, shallots and parsley, made more tasty by the addition of a smoked cheese topping and baked in apple juice to keep the trout beautifully moist. Hot Bramley apples with luxurious farmhouse dairy ice cream finish off the meal.

•

STILTON AND PEAR FLAN

LAKELAND TROUT

STIR-BRAISED CARROTS AND CAULIFLOWER
BRUSSELS SPROUTS
CREAMED POTATOES

FLAME ON ICE

STILTON AND PEAR FLAN

150 g (5 oz) plain flour, half white, half wholemeal
75 g (3 oz) butter
30 ml (2 tbs) water
pinch salt
60 ml (4 tbs) semi-skimmed milk
125 g (4 oz) blue Stilton cheese, crumbled
2 eggs, beaten
2 ripe Conference pears
salt and pepper, to taste
parsley, to garnish

PREHEAT THE OVEN to 220°C (425°F) Gas Mark 7. Make pastry, using flour, butter, water and pinch of salt. Chill for 30 minutes, then roll out and use to line a 18 cm (7 in) flan ring. Cook blind for 10 minutes. Turn oven down to 180°C (350°F) Gas Mark 4. Mix together milk, crumbled cheese, eggs and seasoning. Peel and core pears, cut each into 8 and arrange in flan. Pour the cheese mixture over the pears. Cook until set, approximately 20 minutes. Serve warm.

A combination of classical English cheese and fruit, this starter makes an interesting mixture of sweet and savoury.

ELIZABETH WILLIAMS, WILLIAM FARR COMPREHENSIVE SCHOOL, WELTON, LINCOLNSHIRE

LAKELAND TROUT

4 trout, weight approx 275 g (10 oz) each, cleaned
3 shallots or 1 small onion, finely chopped
125 g (4 oz) mushrooms, chopped
rapeseed oil
125 g (4 oz) granary breadcrumbs
15 ml (1 tbs) parsley, chopped
1 egg, beaten
200 ml ($\frac{1}{3}$ pt) pure English apple juice
50 g (2 oz) smoked Cheddar cheese, grated
salt and pepper, to taste

PREHEAT THE OVEN to 200°C (400°F) Gas Mark 6. Rinse trout and pat dry on kitchen towel. Lightly saute the shallots, or onions, and mushrooms in a little oil. Stir in the breadcrumbs and parsley. Remove from the heat and stir in beaten egg. Season with salt and pepper. Fill trout with the stuffing and lay fish in a greased ovenproof dish. Brush the trout with some oil and pour over the apple juice.

Cook for 10–15 minutes, basting with the apple juice from time to time. When the fish are cooked and tender, sprinkle each with some smoked cheese. Serve hot with a crisp green salad.

Stuffed trout is usually best done with fillets so you have no bones to worry about when eating. Choose butterfly fillets (without the head) and simply lay the stuffing on one half and cover with the other.

MARY BURROUGH, COCKERMOUTH SCHOOL, COCKERMOUTH, CUMBRIA

STIR-BRAISED CARROTS AND CAULIFLOWER

1 small cauliflower
225 g (8 oz) carrots
45 ml (3 tbs) rapeseed oil
175 ml (6 fl oz) vegetable stock
fresh thyme and marjoram, chopped

CUT CAULIFLOWER INTO small florets. Thinly slice carrots. Heat the oil in a large frying pan, on high heat. Put the cauliflower and carrots in pan, stir for 2 minutes. Pour in stock, bring to boil. Add herbs, cover and cook at medium heat for 10 minutes, until the vegetables are just tender. Drain and serve.

SANDRA BROWN, GREENSWARD SCHOOL, HOCKLEY, ESSEX

FLAME ON ICE

4 medium Bramley cooking apples
25 g (1 oz) butter
60 ml (4 tbs) demerara sugar
120 ml (4 fl oz) English cider
vanilla Farmhouse dairy ice cream
hazelnuts, roughly chopped, to
  garnish

PREHEAT THE OVEN to 190°C (375°F) Gas Mark 5. Wipe and core the apples. Slit the skin around the middle. Place apples in a well buttered fire-proof dish and spoon demerara sugar into their middles. Add sufficient cider to cover the base of the baking dish. Cover with a buttered sheet of greaseproof paper or foil. Bake for 20–30 minutes, until tender, being careful not to overcook. Place apples on warmed individual dishes and remove skins. Boil the liquid in the base of the dish briskly until reduced to a syrupy consistency. Pour over apples. Top each with a scoop of ice cream and chopped hazelnuts.

GAIL HENRY, LORD DIGBY'S SCHOOL, SHERBORNE, DORSET

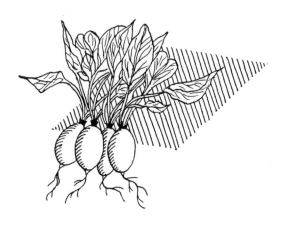

SEASONALITY OF BRITISH PRODUCE

(Dates are approximate, dependent on the weather)

Apples:	
Bramley	All year
Desserts	All year except June according to variety
Artichokes, Globe	June–Sept
Artichokes, Jerusalem	Oct–early spring
Asparagus	May–mid-June
Aubergines	June–Sept
Bacon and Ham	All year
Barley	All year
Basil	April–Oct
Beans:	
Broad	End May–early Sept
French	June–Sept
Runner	Mid-July–Oct
Beef and Veal	All year
Beetroot	All year
Blackberries	Late July till frosts
Blueberries	Mid-July–mid-Oct
Brains (offal)	All year
Broccoli (calabrese)	Mid-June–Nov
and sprouting broccoli	March–May
Brussels sprouts	Late Aug–March
Butter	All year
Cabbage	All year
Capsicums (sweet peppers)	May–Oct
Carrots	All year
Cauliflowers and Cape broccoli	All year
Celeriac	Late Sept–Apr
Celery	Apr–Dec
Cheese	All year
Cherries	Late June–Aug
Chicken	All year
Chicory and radicchio	Mid Apr–mid Nov

Chinese leaf (Chinese leaves or Chinese cabbage)	Mid-Apr–early Jan
Chives	Apr–Oct
Cider	All year
Coriander	Apr–Oct
Courgettes	June–Oct
Cream	All year
Cucumbers	End Jan–Nov
Currants	Sept–early Oct
Damsons	Sept–early Oct
Dill	Apr–Oct
Duck	All year
Eggs	All year
Endive	May–Sept
English hops	Sept
English wine	All year
Farmed venison	All year, mostly Aug–Jan
Feet (offal)	All year
Florence fennel	Aug–Nov
Game	According to shooting seasons
Garlic	With imports, all year
Geese	Mostly Sept–Dec
Goats (produce)	All year
Gooseberries	End May–Aug
Heads (offal)	All year
Hearts (offal)	All year
Horseradish	Apr–Oct
Kale	Nov–May
Kidneys (offal)	All year
Kohl-Rabi	End July–end Feb
Lamb	All year
Leeks	Aug–May
Lettuce	All year

SEASONALITY OF BRITISH PRODUCE

Liver (offal)	All year
Loganberries	Early July–late Aug
Marjoram	Apr–Oct
Marrows (vegetable marrows)	Apr–Oct, peak Aug–Sept
Milk	All year
Mint	Apr–Oct
Mooli	Aug–Oct
Mushrooms	All year
Mutton	All year
Oats	All year
Onions and shallots	Nearly all year round, peak Sept–Apr
Oxtail (offal)	All year
Parsley	All year
Parsnips	Aug–Apr

Pears:
Culinary (Conference) End Sept–end May
Dessert (eg Comice) End Aug (Comice end Oct) –end May, depending on weather

Peas:
Garden May–Oct, peak July
Mange tout July–Sept

Plums	End July–early Oct
Pork	All year
Potatoes	All year: new start late May
Pumpkins and squashes	Late summer–winter
Quince	Oct–Nov
Rabbit (domesticated)	All year
Radishes	Aug–Oct
Rapeseed oil	All year
Raspberries	Late June–Oct
Rhubarb	Dec–June
Rosemary	Apr–Oct
Sage	Apr–Oct
Salmon (farmed)	All year
Salsify	Oct–late spring
Scorzonera	Autumn and winter
Seakale	Nov–spring
Sheep (produce)	All year
Spinach	March–June; Sept–Oct

Strawberries	Mostly May–Oct
Sunberries	Early July–late Aug
Sugar beet (sugar)	All year
Swedes	Sept–May
Sweetbreads (offal)	All year
Sweetcorn	Late July–Oct
Tarragon	Apr–Oct
Tayberries	Early July–mid-Aug
Thyme	Apr–Oct
Tomatoes	March–Nov, peak summer
Tongue (offal)	All year
Tripe (offal)	All year
Trout (farmed)	All year
Tummelberries	Mid July–late Aug
Turkey	All year
Turnips	All year
Watercress	All year, peak Apr–July
Wheat (flour)	All year
Yogurt	All year

INDEX

Almonds
  Toasted, with
    calabrese 86
Angus beef and
  venison pie with
  parsnips 73
Apple
  Autumn pudding 64
  Baked, cheesecake 77
  Betty 60
  Blackberry and,
    meringue basket 66
  Bramble and
    meringue 80
  Chicken and,
    parcels 85
  Clovelly, and celery
    salad 89
  Devonshire fruit
    parcels 89
  Flame on ice 92
  Fruit crisp 67
  Gooseberry and,
    amber 61
  Honeyed,
    cheesecake 83
  Pork with, and cider
    sauce 69
  Smoked mackerel
    with 23
  Spiced, whip 65
  Sweet invicta 62
Asparagus
  East Anglian turkey
  breasts with 37
Autumn pudding 64

Baby corn cob flowers 24
Baked apple
  cheesecake 77
Beef
  and, vegetable
    casserole 41
  Angus, venison pie
    with parsnips 73
  Olives with
    mushroom
    stuffing 39
  Stew with celery and
    walnuts 40
Bideford pears with
  Devonshire
  clotted cream 71
Blackberry and apple
  meringue basket 66

Bramble mushrooms
  with garlic sauce 26
Broccoli (calabrese) 26
  Broccoli mimosa 70
  Calabrese with
    toasted almonds 86
Brussels sprouts with
  hazelnut butter 57

Calabrese (broccoli)
  Broccoli mimosa 70
  with toasted
    almonds 86
Carrots
  Glazed Derry 77
  Julienne, with
    chopped parsley 80
  Stir-braised, and
    cauliflower 92
  with lemon and
    mint 71
  Zesty 56
Casseroles
  Beef and vegetable 41
  Lincolnshire lamb 44
Cauliflower
  Stir-braised carrots
    and 92
Celery
  Beef stew with, and
    walnuts 40
  Chicken in, sauce 82
  Clovelly apple and,
    salad 89
Cheesecake
  Baked apple 77
  Honeyed apple 83
  Raspberry 86
  Ulster 62
Cheese carousel 24
Cheshire
  Cutlets 45
  Mushroom and,
    scallops 69
Chicken
  and apple parcels 85
  and sweetcorn soup 18
  Breasts with ginger
    and garlic 30
  Cumbrian fare 18
  Curried, and yogurt
    plait 34
  Honey barbecued 31
  Humberside,
    breasts 33
  in celery sauce 82

Savoury 29
Stuffed breasts 32
Therese 36
with yogurt 35
Cider
  Roast rabbit in 47
  Pork with apple,
    and sauce 69
Clovelly apple and
  celery salad 89
Cod
  Fish cobbler 51
  Norfolk fish pie 52
  Scallop surprise 20
  Vegetable and fish
    kebabs 21
Corn
  Baby, cob flowers 24
  Chicken and
    sweetcorn soup 20
  Cream of, soup 85
Cream of Corn Soup 85
Cream
  Devonshire clotted,
    with Bideford
    pears 71
Cullen skink 20
Cumbrian fare 19
Curd cheese
  and pears 27
Curried chicken and
  yogurt plait 34

Delia's country
  surprise 76
Devonshire fruit
  parcels 89
Duchesse potatoes 83
Duck
  Lincolnshire roast,
    with stuffing 38

East Anglian turkey
  breasts with
  asparagus 37
Eggs
  Susan's stuffed 88

Fish
  and vegetable
    kebabs 21
  Cobbler 51
  Norfolk, pie 52
Flame on ice 92
Flan
  Stilton and pear 91

Fruit crisp 67

Garlic
  and ginger with
    chicken breasts 30
  Roast potatoes 70
  Sauce, with breaded
    mushrooms 26
Glazed Derry carrots 77
Gooseberry
  and apple amber 61
  Sauce, and grilled
    herring 50
Gravy
  Pigeon breasts in 48
Grilled herring and
  gooseberry sauce 50

Haddock
  Crumble 76
  Cullen skink 19
  Harvest soup 15
Herring
  Grilled with
    gooseberry sauce 50
Honey barbecued
  chicken 31
Honeyed apple
  cheesecake 83
Humberside chicken
  breasts 33

Julienne carrots with
  chopped parsley 80

Kebabs
  Vegetable and fish 21
Kentish delight 40
Kentish potatoes 86

Lakeland trout 91
Lamb
  Cheshire cutlets 45
  Laversdale 79
  Lincolnshire,
    casserole 44
  Welsh, crumble 44
Laversdale lamb 79
Layered onions and
  potatoes 56
Leek and potato soup 79
Lemon
  and mint, with
    carrots 71
Lincolnshire lamb
  casserole 44

INDEX

Lincolnshire roast duck
  with stuffing   38
Liver Valence   46

Mackerel
  Smoked with apple   23
Meringue
  Blackberry and
    apple, basket   66
  Bramble and apple   80
Mint
  and lemon with
    carrots   71
Mushrooms
  and Cheshire
    scallops   69
  Beef olives with,
    stuffing   39
  Breaded with garlic
    sauce   26
  Pate   25

Norfolk fish pie   52

Onions
  Layered, and
    potatoes   56

Pancakes
  Verwood vegetable,
    with Cheddar
    cheese sauce   88
Parsnips
  Croquettes   55
  with angus beef and
    venison pie   73
Pate
  Mushroom   25
  Smokie, with
    oatcakes   73
  Vinney, with pears   28
Pea
  Fresh garden, in
    potato nests   80
  Shropshire, soup   82
Pears
  and curd cheese   27
  and pork   43
  Bideford, with
    Devonshire
    clotted cream   71
  Devonshire fruit
    parcels   43
  Pudding   63
  Stilton and, flan   91
  Vinney pate with   28
Pies
  Angus beef and
    venison   73
  Norfolk fish   52

Strabane vegetable   53
Pigeon breasts in gravy   48
Pork
  and pears   43
  Kentish delight   41
  Wiltshire plait   42
  with apple and cider
    sauce   69
Potatoes
  Duchesse   83
  Garlic roast   70
  Kentish   86
  Layered onions and   56
  Leek and, soup   79
  Nests with fresh
    garden peas   80
  Scalloped   58

Rabbit
  Roast, in cider   47
Raspberry cheesecake   86
Roast rabbit in cider   47

Salads
  Clovelly apple and
    celery salad   89
  Cumbrian fare   17
  Delia's country
    surprise   76
  Vegetarian sunburst   58
  Winter   59
Sauces
  Apple and cider,
    with pork   69
  Celery, with chicken   82
  Cheddar cheese,
    with Verwood
    vegetable
    pancakes   88
  Garlic, with
    breaded
    mushrooms   26
  Gooseberry, and
    grilled herring   50
  Watercress, with
    trout   49
Savoury chicken   29
Scallop surprise   20
Scalloped potatoes   58
Shrimps baked in sour
    cream   22
Shropshire pea soup   82
Smoked mackerel with
    apple   23
Smoked trout pate   22
Smokie pate with
    oatcakes   73
Soup
  Chicken and
    sweetcorn   18

Cream of corn   85
Harvest   15
Leek and potato   79
Shropshire pea   82
Tomato   16
Vegetable and bean   17
Spiced apple whip   65
Spinach roulade   54
Stew
  Beef, with celery
    and walnuts   40
Stilton and pear flan   91
Stir-braised carrots and
    cauliflower   92
Strabane vegetable pie   53
Stuffed chicken breasts   32
Stuffing
  Lincolnshire roast
    duck with   38
Susan's stuffed eggs   88
Sweetcorn
  Baby, cob flowers   24
  Chicken and, soup   18
  Cream of, soup   85
Sweet invicta   62

Tayberry fool   74
Tomato soup   16
Trout
  Hazelnut   50
  Lakeland   91
  Smoked, pate   22
  with watercress
    sauce   49
Turkey
  East Anglian turkey
    breasts with
    asparagus   37

Ulster cheesecake   62

Vegetable
  and bean soup   17
  and fish kebabs   21
  Beef and, casserole   41
  Strabane vegetable
    pie   53
  Verwood, pancakes   88
  Winter salad   58
Vegetarian sunburst
    salad   58
Venison
  Angus beef and
    venison pie with
    parsnips   73
Verwood vegetable
    pancakes with
    Cheddar cheese
    sauce   88
Vinney pate with pears   28

Walnuts
  Beef stew with, and
    celery   40
Watercress
  Sauce, with trout   49
Welsh lamb crumble   44
Wiltshire plait   42
Winter salad   59

Yogurt
  Plait, and curried
    chicken   34
  with chicken   32

Zesty carrots   56